Young Ladies of Character:
Restoring the Princess Ministry

Curriculum
Facilitator's Guide

Kimberly A. Williams, L.M.S.W.

Halo ●●●●
Publishing International
www.halopublishing.com

For additional memorabilia, email author at:
psalms139.14ylc@yahoo.com

Find out more information at:
http://www.YLCPrincess.weebly.com

Library of Congress Control Number: 2009939978
ISBN 978-1-935268-27-7

Author: Kimberly Williams
Illustrator: Kim Sponaugle

Attention Organizations, buyers and educational institutions:

Quantity discounts are available on bulk purchases of this book for reselling, educational purposes, subscription incentives or fund raising. Please contact our Sales Department at 216-255-6756.

Halo ●●●●
Publishing International
www.halopublishing.com

Printed in the United States of America

Acknowledgements

The *Young Ladies of Character: Restoring the Princess Curriculum* has been a true labor of love and commitment. With the completion of this curriculum, I would like to thank the many people who have contributed to the successful launching and longevity of this ministry. I would be remiss if I did not pause for a moment to thank my Lord and Savior Jesus Christ for this divine ministry vision given to me in April, 2004, when the ministry title, vision, and purpose became clear. My parents, Pernell and Georgia Williams provided me with limitless support. Their prayers and personal guidance were priceless. They are my heart.

With much prayer and preparation, this ministry was presented and received in 2005 by Pastor Subash Cherian, Senior Pastor of Highland Church. Pastor Cherian has shown his fervent support of the ministry by allowing us to assemble regularly and host events that were once unique to Highland Church. Minister Karen Weinburg, Highland Church Ministry Liaison in 2005, was also supportive and provided great wisdom and advisement throughout the life of this ministry at Highland Church. Minister Emmanuella Young, Highland Church Youth Minister was not only supportive but attended all events hosted by the ministry. The Intercessors of Prayer at Highland Church are due a spiritual thank you for their many prayers and blessings over our ministry, our events, and all our members throughout the years.

The Young Ladies of Character is a ministry of much excitement and enthusiasm. However, it took time and dedication to shape the ministry into what it has become. I would like to thank Pamela Damon for helping to build the ministry from its beginning. Ms. Damon contributed to the feminine beauty and detail of the ministry. She sacrificed time and energy to make each session and event special and memorable. Thank you.

A distinct thank you is extended to the Frances C. Peterson Foundation and Dr. Frances Peterson for the foundation's tremendous contribution in the form of a grant. This grant made this vision of divine excellence come to fruition. Dr. Peterson graced us with her presence at numerous events and participated in our Presentation Ceremony. Her elegance and grace was admired by many, especially our Princesses.

And yes, our *Princesses*. Thank you to the many parents who supported the ministry throughout the years. Our Princess Parents provided a subtle encouragement to their daughters to determine their interest in this unique ministry. Our parents followed our calendar of events, paid attention to our mailings, attended our events and fundraisers, and volunteered time when requested. A special thanks to Barbera Bethea, Poetry Therapist, for her parenting workshops designed to provide support for the parenting experience. And to all our Princesses who made a commitment to become a ministry member, attend ministry conferences, complete ministry sessions, work to raise funds for the ministry and endure arduous preparation and practices, thank you. For your youthful insight, ministry testimonies, advertisement, and desire to continue returning, thank you!

A special thank you is extended to Inspiration of Writers' editor Sandy Tritt for her gentle guidance and knowledgeable advisement. Her biblical understanding and professional direction provided for a perfect combination in formatting this curriculum to maintain its uniqueness while making precise alterations for the eye and interest of the reader.

A final extension of gratitude to Kim Sponaugle for capturing the exquisite detail of our ministry symbols and colors displayed on the cover.

Thank you.

About the Author

Kimberly A. Williams, an individual and family counselor, mental health trainer, and certified mediator, has worked with the youth population since 2000 with such organizations as the YMCA of NYC, Queens Child Guidance Center, Big Brothers Big Sisters of NYC (as a Mentor for at-risk youth), and East River Child Development Center (assessing the needs of autistic children). Some of Ms. Williams' certifications consist of, but are not limited to, Identification and Reporting of Child Abuse and Maltreatment, School Violence Prevention and Intervention, Sexual Abuse Training for Child Welfare Workers, NYC Administration for Children Services: Healthy Development of Children and Youth. She now works as the District-wide School Social Worker of South Country Central School District in Suffolk County, NY. In this position she serves students from elementary through high school, where she specializes in the area of Homeless and Unaccompanied Youth.

Ms. Williams has an extensive history working with the NYS Court System as parent educator and mediator. She currently volunteers as a facilitator for the Parent Education and Custody Effectiveness (P.E.A.C.E.) program in Suffolk County Supreme Court. The P.E.A.C.E. Program is designed to educate parents about the harmful effects of exposing children to high conflict as a result of the divorce process. The mental health component of this training educates parents about the stages of child development and empowers them to provide their children with a healthy, loving home even when faced with the trials of divorce or separation. Ms. Williams acted as the Program Administrator Coordinator and Facilitator of this program from 2006 through 2007 in Queens County and Bronx County Supreme Court in NYC through Community Mediation Services, Inc.

At Community Mediation Services in Jamaica, NY, an incorporation closely associated with the Family Court System, Ms. Williams worked intensively with at risk youth and families. Through CMS, Ms. Williams received her certification as a Mediator in New York State. While working at CMS, she conducted several mediations and wrote agreements in the area of community disputes, custody and visitation cases, and civil court disputes. Ms. Williams continues to use her mediation skills to resolve conflict within the many systems with which she gives her time.

Ms. Williams received her graduate degree from Fordham University School of Social Service with a clinical concentration and a specialization in children and families, and currently practices as a Licensed Professional. She was nominated for the National Association of Social Workers (NASW) Award in 2006. She graduated magna cum laude from York College with a Bachelor of Science Degree in Social Work. Ms. Williams has been the Ministry Leader of the *Young Ladies of Character: Restoring the Princess Ministry* since 2005, and is a living testament of spiritual living and maximizing one's potential in life. Her desire is that this ministry will go forth and continue to richly impact the lives of young ladies globally.

Y. L. C.

Table of Contents

FACILITATOR GUIDE

MENTORING SESSIONS

Y. L. C.

Introduction to
The Young Ladies of Character: Restoring the Princess Ministry

by Kimberly Williams, L.M.S.W.

This ministry is designed to teach young ladies how to a live a lifestyle based upon biblical standards. It teaches young ladies the importance of basing their self-esteem upon what the Bible says versus what the world says. The first twelve sessions, taught to the *Princess Sisters*, are based upon the Book of Esther. The second six sessions, taught to the *Princess Mentors in Training*, are based upon the Book of Ruth. It's acknowledged that times do change, and cultural perspectives are different; however, all materials were written with detailed sensitivity to female teenagers. As participants make a commitment to attend this ministry, it's important they understand what the ministry is about through the ongoing reading of the ministry's vision. As the sessions are taught, it's important to address the challenges experienced by each participant. It's preferable that these challenges are addressed within the group, but if they are too sensitive or too mature for the group, they should be addressed with the Ministry Leader and another trusted adult. Completion of these sessions should result in each participant feeling accepted and special—that they are the *BEST* and *ONLY* version of themselves and God made them just the way they are. They are not a mistake; they are God's Princesses.

This ministry can be taught in a religious institution, a school setting that allows for biblical teachings, or in a home that is determined to be safe for young people to gather on a consistent basis. It's recommended that an adult who is knowledgeable in the Bible and has experience working with young ladies facilitates these sessions. Princess Leaders-in-Training can co-facilitate sessions once they have met the ministry requirements (*See Ministry Member Titles*). Copies of the curriculum are available for $32.99 each. Ministry Member Pins displaying the ministry logo, which are distributed during Session #6, can be ordered; prices vary based upon quantity. Ministry Certificates can be ordered in quantities of 20 for $30.00. To order copies of this book and accompanying memorabilia, email your request to psalms139.14ylc@yahoo.com. A portion of the proceeds of each curriculum sold will go to a college scholarship fund to encourage all Princesses to continue their education.

Y. L. C.

- ➢ **Ministry Facilitors**: _____, _____

- ➢ **Ministry:** *Young Ladies of Character: "Restoring the Princess Ministry"*

- ➢ **Ministry Members:** *Young ladies eleven to approximately eighteen years of age (Max 21yrs. depending on the need).*

- ➢ **Vision:** *Young ladies will learn how to handle everyday issues of life based upon the word of God. They will learn the importance of seeking a closer and more intimate relationship with Jesus Christ. Young ladies will learn to value their youth, integrity, and maximize their education, and God-given gifts by working towards a character of excellence.*

- ➢ **Meetings**: *The ministry will meet twice a month, for a total of twelve sessions. Each interactive session is two hours in length and consists of Bible-based discussions. Topics include but are not limited to: building self esteem; appropriate attire; creating positive friendships; dating; drugs; manners; and beauty. These meetings are designed to foster healthy relationships, creative thinking, "God-esteem," self-confidence, self-awareness and a deeper love for God.*

- ➢ **Registration:** *Registration begins _____.*

- ➢ **Princess Presentation:** *Annual Presentation Ceremony and Princess Royal Ball*

If you are interested in receiving further information regarding this ministry, email us at *psalms139.14ylc@yahoo.com*

I will praise thee; for I am fearfully and wonderfully made: marvelous are thy works; and that my soul knoweth right well. Psalms 139:14

Y. L. C.

Ministry Symbolisms & Meanings

Ministry Colors:
Pink and Purple represent the feminine design of a lady and her royal ancestry as God's Princess.

White and Gold represent Christ-like purity, value and wealth.

Ministry Pin:
A pin presented when the Young Lady has successfully completed a total of six ministry sessions and is recognized as a Ministry Member.

Glass Shoe:
Symbolizes the Young Lady has committed to learning the importance of allowing God to order her footsteps and is willing to make a public declaration to continue in her walk with Jesus Christ.

Presentation Ceremony:
This spiritual ceremony will allow each Young Lady of Character to make a personal commitment to maintain a lifestyle that is pleasing to God and to continue building her personal relationship with Jesus Christ.

Princess Walks Down the Aisle:
This ceremony represents that the Young Lady of Character is entering into a more mature relationship with God, symbolically walking into her future.

Y. L. C.

Royal Attire:
The Young Lady of Character attends the Presentation Ceremony wearing her best attire; a feminine representation of her beauty is due.

Rhinestone Pin:
This memento is presented to the Young Lady of Character upon completion of the first twelve ministry sessions.

Princess Tiara:
The Young Lady of Character receives this Royal Head Covering at the Presentation Ceremony as recognition of her commitment to Christ.

Bible Distribution:
The Young Lady of Character receives a Bible at the Presentation Ceremony for the purpose of encouraging her to read the Word of God and grow in her knowledge of Jesus Christ.

Princess Royal Ball:
The Young Ladies of Character will celebrate their spiritual commitment to Christ along with friends and family through fellowship, food, and jubilant praise.

Princess Escorts:
Adults who have played an important role in the life of a Princess and are requested to escort their Princess into the Royal Ball.

Y. L. C.

Ministry Member Titles

➢ **Ministry Leader/Facilitator:** Appointed ministry leader embodying a Christian relationship with God, a genuine care for young ladies, and the ability to lead with loving compassion, Godly insight, and strength.

➢ **Princess Sister:** Members of the Young Ladies of Character Ministry.

➢ **Princess Mentor-in-Training:** Young Lady of Character Princesses who have successfully completed twelve ministry sessions and the Presentation Ceremony.

➢ **Princess Mentor:** Young Ladies of Character Princesses who have completed all eighteen ministry sessions and are ready to begin mentoring their Princess Sisters.

➢ **Princess Leader-in-Training:** Young Lady of Character Princesses who have completed a minimum of two years of ministry and who demonstrate spiritual maturity and Christian leadership. Although maturing, this Princess should provide a Christian example of youthful living. This Princess should begin co-facilitating ministry sessions.

Y. L. C.

Ministry Culture

The Young Ladies of Character: Restoring the Princess Ministry was created to establish healthy, lasting relationships between its members. Regardless of their backgrounds, young ladies should feel welcomed and comfortable as a part of a group designed to enhance their relationship with God, their self-esteem, and their growth into a well-rounded individual. The *Princess Greeting*, in which a Princess delicately grasps the right hand of another Princess and gently kisses her on each cheek, fosters this welcoming atmosphere. This special greeting also establishes a sense of togetherness.

Young Ladies of Character members should be encouraged to take ownership of their ministry through participation and inclusion in decisions appropriate to their level of maturity. Ministry Leaders/Facilitators should convey the message that their ministry will be as great as the young ladies who participate in it. In order to build trust and a comfort level amongst ministry members, a closed door policy should be established following the completion of Session #1.

Each Princess Session should begin and end with the *Princess Prayer Stance*, in which all Princesses assemble in a circle and delicately lock arms. Ministry Leader/Facilitator should explain the purpose of the locking of arms, which is a representation of not allowing anything between them as they pray. Princesses should be encouraged to lead in all prayers or recite a prayer at the completion of the session.

Annual Princess Trips and Events

All trips associated with the Young Ladies of Character: Restoring the Princess Ministry should be designed to expose its members to activities that are both fun and educational. The Ministry Leader/Facilitator is encouraged to expose their Princesses to unique attractions.

Annual Princess Fundraisers

Young Ladies of Character: Restoring the Princess Ministry Fundraisers should maintain a reflection of the ministry vision. Creative ideas such as a Princess High Tea Luncheon, Career Day, Fashion Show, Talent Show, etc. are suggested in Ministry Events. The monies received from all fundraisers should be used for the enrichment of the ministry members and maintenance of a standard of excellence.

Princess Chats

At the completion of Session #12, the Ministry Leader/Facilitator will speak with each Princess individually about her personal growth and challenges. This conversation should address each Princess' spiritual growth, self-esteem, lifestyle, and ability to set an example for others. Ministry Leader/Facilitator will use these chats to determine the Princess's ability to move up to the next level in ministry.

Princess Parents' Meeting

At the completion of the ministry year, the Ministry Leader/Facilitator will coordinate a mandatory parents' meeting. Ministry Leader/Facilitator will use this opportunity to speak with all Princess parents in a group format. All Ministry Leader/Facilitator statements should be general in nature and apply to all Princesses. If there are challenges with a particular Princess, the situations should be addressed at the time they occur. Do not wait to address these challenges at the Princess Parents' Meeting, as it's important that parents do not feel afraid or intimidated by this meeting. Inform parents of details regarding their daughters' level within ministry, Princess Presentation Ceremony and Royal Ball, as well as required rehearsals. The Ministry Leader/Facilitator should strive to make this meeting informational as well as interesting through activities such as *Reflections* or by inviting a special guest speaker.

Annual Princess Presentation Ceremony and Royal Ball
Rehearsals

1st Rehearsal
Ministry Leaders will lead Princesses in practicing for Princess Presentation Ceremony. The ceremony consists of a processional, curtsy, rhinestone pinning, tiara crowning of Princesses, Bible distribution, brief sermon, reciting of Covenant Prayer, and recessional.

2nd Rehearsal
The Princess Royal Ball (formal affair) consists of a processional, distribution of Young Ladies of Character: Restoring the Princess Ministry Certificates, curtsy and seating. During this rehearsal, Princesses should be reminded of ministry sessions focused on etiquette and manners.

Summer Break

The Young Ladies of Character: Restoring the Princess Ministry is structured to meet twice a month for a year, with a two month break provided in the summer for family time. The ministry year ends with the Annual Presentation Ceremony.

Y.L.C.

Ministry Registration Form

The Young Ladies of Character: Restoring the Princess Ministry is excited about helping you get a better understanding about who you are as a young lady. We also look forward to seeing you grow in your relationship with God.

By signing below you agree to attend each Princess Session. If you must be absent, you agree to call your Ministry Leader. You also commit to reading the Book of Esther by Session 6, and agree to play an active part in each Princess Session.

Princess Information:

Date: _____

Name: _____Age:_____

Princess Address: _____

Princess Email Address: _____

Home#: _____ Cell#:_____

Princess Parent/Guardian's Information:

Name: _____

Home#:_____ Cell#: _____

Email Address: _____

Vision: Young ladies will learn how to handle everyday issues of life based upon the word of God. They will learn the importance of maximizing their education and seeking a closer and more intimate relationship with Jesus Christ, while also learning the value of their youth, integrity, and God-given talents.

Y. L. C.

REGISTRATION SURVEY

Age: _____

Welcome to the ***Young Ladies of Character: Restoring the Princess Ministry***! This ministry was created to restore the Princess in you. It was designed to focus on all the areas in your life that are important to you. Please help us get to know you better by answering the questions below. Please answer the questions honestly and anonymously (do *NOT* write your name on this form).

Please complete this survey and return it to your Ministry Leader.

How did you hear about this ministry?

What do you expect you will get or learn by attending this ministry?
List three topics you think are important to talk about during your ministry sessions:

1.

2.

3.

List two things that you like to do:

1.

2.

Who do you look up to? Why?

Have you asked Jesus to come into your heart/life?

Are you ready to become ***A Young Lady of Character, a True Princess***? Why?

LET'S TALK ABOUT IT!

12 Sessions of Princess Chats

Princess Rules

Friendship   Spirit of Giving

Establishing Trust

Women of the Bible   STYLE

Fashion

Forgiveness

EDUCATION   **True Happiness**

Wanting to Belong, Be Loved

Health and Hygiene

Loving Jesus

Self-Esteem

Beauty   Appropriate Attire

Sex   Career and Development   *Fashion Do's & Don'ts*

Dating

DEPRESSION

Relating to Parents   Church   DRUGS

EXCELLENCE!   **LEADERSHIP**

Y. L. C.

PARENT PERMISSION SLIP

I, _____ the parent/guardian of _____, give my child permission to attend The Young Ladies of Character: Restoring the Princess Ministry. I understand the ministry will meet twice a month on Saturdays for a series of 12 sessions. I also understand that the ministry will discuss many topics that concern adolescent girls and young ladies that may include sex, drugs, and depression; these serious topics will be addressed from a biblical perspective.

If you have concerns or questions feel free to contact
_____.

Parent/Guardian Name: _____
(print)

Complete Mailing Address: _____

_____

Phone #: _____ Cell #: _____

Emergency Contact #: _____, _____
(Name)   (Number)

Does your daughter have any allergies or disabilities we should be aware of? Please state:
_____
Is there any activity that your daughter will not be allowed to participate in? Please state:

_____

Daughter's Complete Name: _____
Daughter's Birth Date: _____

PARENT/GUARDIAN SIGNATURE: _____

Y. L. C.

EMERGENCY CONTACT FORM
Ministry Leader/Facilitator Copy
(*Please carry this document on all ministry trips*)

Princess Full Name: _____

Princess Date of Birth: _____

Telephone #: _____ Cell #: _____

Home Address: _____

Email Address: _____

Allergies: _____

Parent/Guardian's Full Name/s: _____

Parent/s' Cell #: _____ or _____

Parent/s' Email Address: _____

Emergency Contacts: _____ _____
                               (Name)   (Contact #)

Princess Emergency Form
Princess Copy
(*Please keep this information on you during this trip*)

Trip Location: (Name) _____
                 (Address) _____
                 (Phone #) _____

Ministry Leader: _____ _____
                   (Name)   (Cell #)
Chaperone: _____ _____
                (Name)   (Cell #)
Church/Organization #: _____

Reflections
Parenting Workshop

**Instructions: Think about the questions listed below, and then answer them.
Be prepared to share some of your answers with the group.**

Remember when you were 14 years old?

1.   What were some of the most important things to you?

2.   Who were the most important people to you, and why?

3.   What did you think about the opposite sex?

4.   How did you feel about your parents?

5.   How did you feel about yourself?

6.   What were you the most insecure about?

7.   What was YOUR style (hair, clothes, and accessories)?

8.   What were two things you got in trouble for?

9.   What did you think about God/Church?

10. Is it possible that your daughter/daughters may be experiencing some of the same feeling you had as a young person?

Y. L. C.

MINISTRY CALENDAR

YEAR: _____

Church/Organization: _____

Introduction Session: Getting to Know You	September	Rm # ___
Session #1	September	Rm # ___
Session #2	October	Rm # ___
Session #3	October	Rm # ___
Session #4	November	Rm # ___
Session #5	November	Rm # ___
Session #6	December	Rm # ___
BREAK FOR THE HOLIDAYS		
Session #7	January	Rm# ___
Session #8	February	Rm# ___
Session #8B	February	Rm # ___
High Tea Event Preparation Session	March	Rm# ___
High Tea Set-Up: Décor & Table Setting	March	Dining Hall (6 – 9 p.m.)
Princess High Tea	March	Dining Hall
Session #9	April	Rm # ___
Session #10	April	Rm# ___
Session #11	May	Rm# ___
Career Day Set-Up	May	Open Space
Career Day	May	Open Space
Session #12	June	Rm# ___
Parents Meeting/1st Rehearsal	June	Rm# ___ & Chapel
2nd Rehearsal	July	Open Space
Presentation Ceremony & Royal Ball	July	Church & Dining Hall
SUMMER BREAK		

Ministry Events

TASK ASSIGNMENT'S

Dear Princesses,

Your time has come. This is your first opportunity to present yourselves as Young Ladies of Character—young ladies who understand who you are in Christ and who have learned how to conduct yourselves as ladies. All the tasks on this sheet are important. Please take some time to read them and decide the way in which you would like to minister.

Keep in mind that everything we do must be done in love. So choose a role you will enjoy. **AND REMEMBER, YOU MUST BE COMMITTED TO FULFILLING YOUR RESPONSIBILITY.**

1. Decorators (6)

Duties/Responsibilities: Be available on (date) _____ at (time) _____. Decorate tables and chairs; arrange food and pastries on platters. Must be prepared to work, follow instructions, and think creatively. *Be prepared to transform our chosen location into a room of beauty fit for royalty.*

Attributes: Must be organized. Have a sense of style & creativity.

2. Greeters (2)

Duties/Responsibilities: Greet and welcome guests at the door with a friendly smile (*ex. "Good afternoon, welcome to our Princess High Tea Luncheon"*). Provide seating instructions, if needed. Distribute High Tea Programs.

Attributes: Must have a servant's attitude with a friendly smile.

3. Ushers (2)

Duties/Responsibilities: Escort guests to tables and pull out chairs for them. Fill front tables first.

Attributes: Must seat guests with a smile and answer any questions asked.

4. Servers (8)

Duties/Responsibilities: Attend to two tables. Walk while holding serving trays, teapot, and other beverages or finger foods. Ask guests how they are doing, whether they are in need of anything (such as refills of tea or water). Know ahead of time the location of restrooms. Monitor assigned tables and refer any questions you can't answer to the Ministry Leader/Facilitator.

Attributes: Must have a servant's attitude with a friendly smile, a good memory, and the ability to remain calm under pressure. Must also like to help people.

5. Kitchen Staff (4 – 2 Dish Washers; 2 Dish Dryers)

Duties/Responsibilities: Remove plates and tableware from tables. Wash and dry tableware. Provide clean plates for servers when needed. Maintain a smooth-running and calm kitchen.

Attributes: Must be very organized, enjoy teamwork, value cleanliness, and not mind working behind the scenes.

6. Princesses Hostesses (5)

Duties/Responsibilities: Exemplify appropriate table manners for guests. Greet guests at tables and answer any questions about the ministry. Help distribute any materials. Mingle with guests when appropriate.

Attributes: Must be friendly and calm.

7. High Tea Facilitator (1)

Duties/Responsibilities: Speak on microphone throughout the luncheon. Welcome guests, introduce the day's events, announce upcoming events, and introduce members. Maintain a smile throughout the day.

Attributes: Must be comfortable with public speaking and being in the spotlight.

8. Princess Registration Table (2)

Duties/Responsibilities: Check off names on the High Tea Attendance List and receive money as guests arrive. You must be able to tell guests what the Young Ladies of Character Ministry is all about (know the Ministry Vision in your own words). Take contact information of young ladies interested in joining our ministry when the next year of sessions begins. Keep the flow of getting contact information and distributing materials running smoothly.

Attributes: Must have neat penmanship, enjoy talking to people, and have good organizational skills.

9. Princess DJ (2)

Duties/Responsibilities: Keep music playing throughout the event; keep system safe.

Attributes: Must have a friendly personality, but able to be assertive if necessary.

Young Ladies of Character
Career Day

Y. L. C.

Print your name. Under your name, list two professions that you are interested in.
(Do <u>not</u> list career choices more than once.)

Name _____   Name _____

    1. _____   1. _____

    2. _____   2. _____

Name _____   Name _____

    1. _____   1. _____

    2. _____   2. _____

Name _____   Name _____

    1. _____   1. _____

    2. _____   2. _____

Name _____   Name _____

    1. _____   1. _____

    2. _____   2. _____

Name _____   Name _____

    1. _____   1. _____

    2. _____   2. _____

Young Ladies of Character:
Restoring the Princess Ministry

Career Day
Volunteer Description and Outline

This is an outline for the information we would like you to provide about your career to our career day attendees. Please put job description, opportunities for growth, and pros and cons in paragraph form, and make all information as precise and reader-friendly as possible. Please feel free to add information to provide the most complete description of your career/profession. Thank you.

<u>Title/Name</u>

Career/Educational training:
- Recommended Colleges or Trade Schools
- Time length of training/study
- Brief description of training
- Skills needed to work in field

Entry-level salary range
Salary Range (for example, $20,000-$50,000):

Personal Positive Characteristics/Attributes for those succeeding in this career:

Job description:
- Basic job description
- Average day
- Work environment
- Expected work hours

Opportunity for growth

If you could do it all over again, would you make the same career choice?

Please list pros and cons of this career:

What attracted you to this field?

Young Ladies of Character:
Restoring the Princess Ministry

Career Day
Letter to our Presenter

Dear _____:

On (date) _____ The Young Ladies of Character: Restoring the Princess will host a Career Day
at _____.

This day is designed to educate:

- Youth who are about to graduate from elementary, middle school or high school
- Children who have a dream about what they want to do when they grow-up
- Adults who may have decided to return to school
- Adults who would like to change careers

Therefore, this day is extended to the entire community.

Our goal is to provide a career panel of various professions. Please let us know if you are interested in facilitating one of four workshops ranging from career readiness to the importance of education. Therefore, we have requested that you join us this day to provide information for those interested in your field.

Each volunteer should provide us with a written document consisting of a brief description of each career. We would also like each Career Day Presenter to set up a table consisting of copies of this information, as well as interesting visuals to represent their field.

Please reply as soon as possible so that we may address any questions or concerns you may have.

Thank you.

Sincerely,

Young Ladies of Character:
Restoring the Princess Ministry

Facilitator Guide

This guide is dedicated
To all the
Young Ladies
going through this process of restoration:
You are beautiful inside and out.
Your eyes still sparkle with the innocence of childhood,
yet glow with the woman flourishing within.
Your heart is gentle but strong,
constantly being refined by your Heavenly Father.
Smile and know that you are blessed,
for you are fearfully and wonderfully made.

Kimberly A. Williams, LMSW

Young Ladies of Character: Restoring the Princess Ministry

Date: _____

Princess Sisters	Mentors in Training

Name	Name
1.	1.
2.	2.
3.	3.
4.	4.
5.	5.
6.	6.
7.	7.
8.	8.
9.	9.
10.	10.
11.	11.
12.	12.
13.	13.
14.	14.
15.	15.
16.	16.
17.	17.
18.	18.
19.	19.
20.	20.
21.	21.
22.	22.
23.	23.
24.	24.
25.	25.

Introduction Session: *Getting to Know You*

(Purpose: The Introductory Session is the first meeting held with Princesses. It will allow all attendees an opportunity to get to know one another. Princesses will gain an understanding of the purpose of the ministry and its vision. Princesses will be informed of the ministry requirements and leave with a clearer understanding of what to expect.

AGENDA

Meet and greet
Opening prayer: Princess Prayer Stance (the purpose of locking of arms is discussed)
Welcome and introduction by ministry leaders

STEP #1
Princess Activity: Getting to Know You Memory Game
Each Princess will introduce herself, share something about herself, and repeat the name of the previous Princess and the statement she shared *(EXAMPLE: Hi, my name is Princess Mary and I like to skate, and this is Princess Susan and she likes to eat popcorn).*

Purpose of Ministry: Ministry Leader will explain the ministry's:
- Focus and foundation
- Meaning of symbols
- Meaning of colors & levels
- Meaning of locking of arms
- Princess greeting

STEP #2
Princess Discussion: Ministry Leader will encourage an open discussion about:
- Session topics
- Princess Rules
- Activities
- Attendance
- Bringing Bibles to every session
- Ministry Dues
- Closed Door Policy

Handouts:
Ministry Year Calendar
Parent Consent Forms

Take Home Assignment: Requested Readings
Genesis 1 and the Book of Esther

Closing Prayer

Y. L. C.

Session #1

In the Beginning God's Perfect Creation

Psalms 139:14 (KJV) I will praise thee for I am fearfully and wonderfully made; marvelous are thy works; and that my soul knoweth right well.

Purpose: Princesses will come to an understanding of God's special and unique creation of women. They will learn to appreciate their female gender.

STEP #1
Princess Activity: The Uniqueness of Women
Princesses will stand in a circle facing inward. Ministry Leader will ask Princesses to look at one another, and based upon what they see, share what it is that makes women different from men (POSSIBLE ANSWERS: bodily shape, clothing, beauty, hair style).

Follow-up Questions:
Ministry Leader will ask Princesses what is feminine/femininity and why God made women different than men (POSSIBLE ANSWERS: *man needed a help-meet, God fashioned women with qualities men did not have, women were designed to have children*).

What is the one thing God designed only women to do?
(*Answer: Have children*)

Ministry Leader Insight: *Ministry Leader will encourage Princesses to reflect on the fact that God only gave women the special role of bearing children. Although God created man first, without women, God's creation of mankind would not continue.*

All Princesses repeat three times: I am special.
I am beautiful.
I am a woman.

STEP #2
Genesis 1   *Review entire chapter with particular attention to the detail of God's creation.*

Princess Bible Study:
Ministry Leader will encourage Princesses to read the details of God's creation and share why they think God pays so much attention to detail.

EXAMPLE: **Gen 1:3-6 (NIV)** And God said let there be light. God saw that the light was good, and he separated the light from the darkness. God called the light "day", and the darkness he called "night." And there was evening and there was morning—the first day.

- Why do you think God pays so much attention to detail?
  (POSSIBLE ANSWER: He wants everything to be perfect.)

- What does this say about Gods creation of woman?

- What does this say about Gods creation of YOU?

Read Gen 1:26-28, 31
(Note: God emphasizes that his creation was not just good (as in vs. 25), but very good!)

Ministry Leader Insight: *God took the time to pay attention to every detail of his creation so that it would be just right/perfect! God took the time to create each of us with the same amount of detail. You are God's perfect creation of YOU!*

STEP #3
Princess Discussion: A Princess Look in the Mirror

- What do we say about ourselves when we look in the mirror?

- Do we put ourselves down or call ourselves ugly?

- What do we think about ourselves when people compliment us?
  (Do we think they are wrong? Do we think they are lying? Do we not feel good unless we receive a compliment?)

- Do we think it's okay to compliment others? Why/why not?

Princess Activity:
Materials Needed: Paper, pens or pencils
Distribute paper and pens and ask Princesses to fold the paper into two columns. In one column, Princesses list things they dislike when they look into the mirror or simply dislike about themselves. In the other column, Princesses will list things they like about themselves. Inform Princesses they will not be asked to read their lists aloud—these are their private thoughts.

Follow-up Questions:
Which list is longer?

Are there any GOOD qualities you feel you have that you would like to share?

How do you think God feels when we criticize His perfect creation of YOU?

Purpose: Princesses will recognize how often they put themselves down and how much easier it is to think negative things about themselves than positive things. Princesses will recognize that we are created in the image of God (Genesis 1:26), making us perfect in God's eyes. Princesses will become more comfortable and confident in themselves, realizing that they are a unique, perfect creation.

The Lines of our Hands

Princesses will be asked to look at their palms and describe what they see. Princesses will be encouraged to pay attention to all the lines, dark /light spots, creases, visible veins, bruises, etc. Ministry Leader will explain how a person might look at their hands and focus on all of its imperfections. However, it's important to realize that no two people on earth have the exact same fingerprint. The creases, lines, and marks on our hands may appear as imperfections but are actually a part of our identity; they make us who we are. Princesses should be reminded that this is another example of the detail of God's creation.

Ministry Leader Insight: *When we look at our lives we may see ourselves as imperfect, but God is able to use all of those imperfections for his glory/good. He can take our mistakes and use them to encourage others; our hurts may teach us the importance of enjoying/appreciating our blessings.*

You are God's perfect creation of YOU!

Form Princess Prayer Stance: locking of arms
CLOSING PRAYER: Recited out loud by the entire group.

GOD'S PERFECT DESIGN

Father, I praise you in the name of your Son, Jesus Christ. Lord, I confess my sins to you and know that you are faithful and just to forgive me and cleanse me from all unrighteousness. I come humbly before you, Lord, thanking you for the beautiful creation of me. I thank you for taking so much time to make me into who I am—to put my nose where it is, to place that twinkle in my eye. God, I make a promise to you, to only speak things about myself that are uplifting and encouraging to me. I will compliment your perfect design, called (name) _____. And when I am tempted to think bad thoughts about myself, I will remember that you made me in your image, the image of God. Any mistakes that I have made, I ask you to forgive me, and I forgive myself. I will wake up every morning knowing that:

I am special;
I am beautiful;
I am God's true Princess.
Hallelujah, AMEN.

The Person Looking Back at Me

Partly dressed, no make-up, bows, or barrettes
Looking at myself with lots of regrets.
Look at my small eyes, my big nose, my ugly feet and my crooked toes
If only I had a different shape, hey, why stop there; why not give myself a different face?
I'd slightly move my eyes to give more space to my nose
I would make my hair curly—or straight—who knows?
I'd change my complexion to what's in style
And make my lips into a perfect smile

But the person looking back at me says
I made you look just like me
In my own image I created thee
The perfection of Your Majesty
I numbered every hair on your head
Every dimple on your cheek
Every curve on your hip
And crease in your lip
I know you, I know you, better than you know yourself

Yet you look at me and tell me you don't like what you see
Nine months and more I fashioned you
With all the detail of whom I am
I put in you who you are
Sculpting and shaping, thinking ahead, and remaking
Until you were done, perfectly designed for my will to come
Your smile, for that time you stand on stage,
Your legs, for that race you will win at a young age
That spot on your face, viewed by that special person as beauty
To that funny laugh I gave you that will liven up a room

But you look and say, you don't like what you see
When you see me looking back at thee
Your own image looks back at you
Seeing only the beauty that is you
The Princess that you are created to be
In all MY Royal Majesty
You are beautiful
You are a woman
You are that tender lovely side of ME.

Kimberly A. Williams, LMSW

Session # 2
The Spiritual Love between a King and His Princess

Deuteronomy 33:12 (NIV) About Benjamin he said: "Let the beloved of the Lord rest secure in him, for he shields him all day long, and the one the Lord loves rests between his shoulders."

Purpose: Princesses will reflect on the unconditional love and security of God and how to build a relationship with him. Princesses' self-worth should be increased by understanding how much God loves them unconditionally—and in a different way than man's love.

Preparation: Mark Bible for scripture reading.

STEP #1
Princess Activity: Resting in His Arms

Ministry Leader will request Princesses to stand and pair up. Princesses will take turns resting their heads on fellow Princesses' shoulder. Once Princesses have switched positions, request they remain in position while the Ministry Leader reads the following scripture verse:

Deuteronomy 33:12 (NIV) "Let the beloved of the Lord rest secure in him, for he shields him all day long, and the one the Lord loves rests between his shoulders."

Follow-up Questions:

- How did it feel to rest your head on your Princess' shoulder?
  (ex. nice, comforted, personal, special, weird, etc.)

- How did it feel to have someone rest on your shoulder?
  (ex. loving, caring, special, strange, etc.)

- How does it feel when you rest your head on your parents shoulder?
  (ex. safe, loved, comfortable, special, worry free, etc.)

- How do you think God feels about you if he encourages you to rest your head on his shoulders? *(ex. he loves us, he wants us to feel safe and secure).*

STEP #2
Scripture References: Request Princesses to pick a Bible verse and read aloud:

- **John 1:12-13**
- **John 15:9-11**
- **1 John 4:10**
- **Romans 5:8**
- **Romans 8:38, 39**

Question:
What do all these scripture verses have in common?
(Answer: They speak of God's love for us.)

Princess Reflection: Ministry Leader will read the following reflection and request Princesses to listen and think about it.

How does it make you feel to know that the God who created the UNIVERSE desires to have a close family relationship with you? The God who existed from ETERNITY to ETERNITY desires to call you his *daughter (say it softly).* God, who knows all about your past and present, mistakes and sins still chooses to love you and be close to you. He wants to be your very closest friend.

STEP #3
Princess Discussion: Princess Love and Friendship

Now that God has told us how much he loves us, how do we tell him how much we love him? *(SUGGESTIONS: Tell him every day).*

- Do we see God as our friend? Why or why not?
- How do we build a relationship with a friend?
  (EXAMPLES: Spend time with them; talk to them on the phone; give them gifts; remember special days.)
- How can we build a closer relationship with God?
- What can we do to make God feel special?
  (EXAMPLES: Celebrate him; tell him you love him; obey him; share him with others.)
- How can we learn more about him?
  (EXAMPLES: Prayer; Bible reading.)

Final Activity: A Princess Verse of Love
Materials: Pretty paper & pens
Now that we have read a few scripture verses God wrote expressing his love for us, let's take a few minutes and write a **Princess Verse of Love** expressing our love for God. *Ministry Leader will collect Princess Verses to be distributed during session #3.*

Closing Thought: Your personal relationship with God is the gateway to understanding your true identity. The closer you are to God, the more you will understand yourself. This is because you have a close relationship with someone who knows you better than you know yourself. The more time you spend with your Heavenly Father, the more he will share with you.

At Home Activity:
Each day think of another way to show God you love him. Act on these thoughts, then come back and share the impact this exercise had on your week.

Form Princess Prayer Stance: Locking of arms
Closing Prayer

Y. L. C.

Session # 3

PRICELESS
The Identity of a Princess: Understanding Her Self-Worth

Esther 2:9 (NIV) The girl pleased him and won his favor. Immediately he provided her with beauty treatments and special food. He assigned to her seven maids selected from the king's palace and moved her and her maids into the best place in the harem.

Purpose: Princesses will be reminded of God's love for them and the importance of building an intimate relationship with him. Princesses will begin to appreciate their uniqueness.

STEP #1   *Read: That Special Someone*
                                        (See 4ᵗʰ page of Session #3)

Princess Question: Can we talk to God…
- At school?
- At work?
- At the bus stop?

Princesses should give examples of more places we can talk to God.

Follow-up Question: How can we talk to God in these places?
(SUGGESTIONS: pray in silence; whisper a prayer; find a safe, quiet place)

Ministry Leader Insight: *Ministry Leader will place emphasis on simply talking with God, as this is called prayer. We can talk to God wherever we go and whenever we choose to. God is always interested in spending time with us.*

STEP #2
Princess Time of Sharing: Reflection on Session #2 Take Home Activity
Ministry Leader will ask Princesses to share what they did each day to show God they love Him or how they made God feel special. Ministry Leader will ask Princesses to share how they plan to continue building this friendship with God (SUGGESTIONS: prayer; Bible reading; talking to God throughout the day; poetry).

Princess Activity: My Prayer Corner

Materials Needed: Pink and purple material, blanket or sheet, lace, pillow, worship music, flowers, etc. Ministry Leader will encourage Princesses to use the materials provided to decorate a special corner in the room to share Princess verses with God (created at the end of Session #2). This corner should provide some privacy for the Princesses. After the corner is decorated, the Ministry Leader will distribute the Princess verses and encourage each Princess to visit the corner, read their verse to God, and share a few of their thoughts, concerns, or thankfulness with him.

*Important: As Princesses are having their individual time with God, the Ministry Leader will request remaining Princesses to continue reading **Esther Chapters 1 and 2**. The noise in the room should remain minimal until all Princesses have had a special moment in the Prayer corner.*

Princess Reflections

Ministry Leader will ask Princesses to share what they remember from The Lines on Our Hands Activity. Remind Princesses of previous two sessions in which we focused on our loving relationship with Jesus Christ and how God loves us no matter how many mistakes we have made. God wants us to come to him just as we are and build a great friendship.

STEP #3
Introduce Lesson: The Identity of a Princess

Purpose: This section will encourage all Princesses to look at who they are and understand their personality and unique qualities. Each Princess will begin to see how they each were created to be used by God.

Princess Discussion: Who are YOU?

Ministry Leader will ask Princesses to visualize/imagine that they have just entered a room full of beautiful young women. Ministry Leader will ask Princesses to share what they think would make them unique or stand out among all the women in the room (SUGGESTIONS: Personality, characteristics, style, relationship with Christ).

Ministry Leader Insight: True beauty/identity is not just an outward appearance, but starts from the inside. The way people see us and relate to us is often determined by how we feel about ourselves. Our personal relationship with God is the gateway to understanding our true identity. Figure out who we are through God's word.

Let's look at a young woman who had to come to the understanding of who she was at a young age. And through the trials of her life (lines in our hands), saved a nation.

STEP #4
Princess Bible Study:
Review and Discuss Esther, chapter 1
- What do we know about King Xerxes?
- Why did Queen Vashti refuse to join the King upon his request? Was it self-respect or rebellion? (focus on Esther 1:10,11 "high spirits from wine")
- What happened to Queen Vashti?

Read Esther 2:1-9
Princesses read these verses aloud, and then discuss them, with an emphasis on Esther's favor (vs. 9). Ministry Leader will encourage Princesses to imagine themselves in Esther's place.

Final Thought:
Just as Esther stood out (found favor, vs.9) among a multitude of beautiful virgins, so should we stand out because of Christ living inside of us. The more we grow in Christ, the more beautiful and confident we will become.

Form Princess Prayer Stance: Locking of arms
Closing Prayer

Take Home Assignment: Read the remainder of the book of Esther.

That Special Someone
(Practice this prior to reading)

That Special Someone stood at the side of my bed this morning,
so excited for me to wake up, so excited to say good morning.
The alarm went off; I looked at the clock and jumped out of bed.
I realized I was running late, so I ran right into the bathroom.
That Special Someone thought…
"Well, she's running late. Maybe she'll say hello when she finishes."

Before I finished brushing my teeth, I turned on the shower and jumped right in.
That Special Someone decided to wait for me in my room with the hope that I would simply say good morning.
That Special Someone knows exactly how my day will go.
That Special Someone knows that I will make it to school on time, but my best friend will decide not to wait for me this time.
That Special Someone knows about that surprise test I will have in school, and wants to warn and protect me from that girl who has been picking on me.

But I grab my breakfast sandwich and run out the door.
That Special Someone tries to walk along side of me,
but I run to the bus stop and say hello to my friends.
The bus comes and I get right on, not realizing that the door closes in the face of That Special Someone.

That Special Someone decides to wait for me at the school's front door.
That Special Someone says to Himself,
"I know she will talk to me when she gets inside."
The bus stops, I jump off and run into school, That Special Someone stands there as I walk by.
My first class is soon over, and so is the school day.
My best friend is no longer speaking to me. I almost got into a fight and hid in the bathroom.
Little did I know that my Special Someone kept those mean girls from coming inside.
I run out of the school at the end of the day, jump on the bus, pushing that Special Someone out of the way.

When I get home, I walk right past everyone inside and go straight to my room.
That Special Someone peeks in my room, only to see me crying on the bed.
That Special Someone begins to cry as well, feeling my great sadness, and rubs my head.
Just as that Special Someone begins to talk to me, offering me words of comfort and advice for tomorrow, I fall asleep, and that Special Someone hopes for tomorrow.
That Special Someone now stands at the side of my bed, hoping that tomorrow I will say good morning.

Now ask yourself who is that Special Someone?
That Special Someone is Jesus Christ.

Restoring the Princess Ministry

Y. L. C.

Session #4

Queen Esther: Walking Into Her Purpose

Esther 4:14 (NIV) For if you remain silent at this time, relief and deliverance for the Jews will arise from another place, but you and your father's family will perish. And who knows but that you have come to royal position for such a time as this?

Purpose: Princesses will come to understand the importance of living every moment to the fullest. Princesses will appreciate the blessings in their lives and not take for granted the opportunities received.

STEP #1
Free Writing Icebreaker: This Present Moment
Princesses will write freely for five minutes about this very moment. Not about the past or future, but specifically about this very moment. (How do they feel right now? What do they see in front of them? What is going through their minds?)

Follow-up Question:
Was this an easy activity to do? Why or why not?
Would it have been easier to write about what has already happened or what you are looking forward to? Why?
Why do you think we did an activity focusing on the present?

Ministry Leader Insight: Ministry Leader will challenge Princesses to think about how we often get caught up in the fast pace of life and forget to enjoy the special moments God gives us. Let's take time each day to be in the moment and think about why we are here right now experiencing this very moment.

STEP #2
Princess Bible Study: Discuss the remainder of Esther , chapter 2
    Questions to consider:
* What process of preparation did Esther go through before she was presented to the King?
* What do we learn about Esther's character in Esther 2:15 and 2:20?
* What do you think made Esther win the favor of the King?
* What can we learn from Esther?
* Who was Mordecai, and what secret did he learn?

Discuss the remainder of Esther, chapter 3

Questions to consider:
- Who was Haman?
- How did Mordecai anger Haman?
- What did Haman plot to do?
- What symbol of authority did King Xerxes give to Haman?

STEP #3
Read Esther, chapter 4, aloud

Princess Discussion:
What are the biblical events in the book of Esther that lead up to Mordecai asking Esther to help save the Jews?

Re-read Esther 4:14

- Does it seem as if God specifically chose Queen Esther to save the Jews?
- Could God have chosen someone else for this purpose?
- How do you think Esther felt when Mordecai first told her what he wanted her to do? *(Re-read Esther 4:9-11)*
- What would have happened to the Jews if Esther refused to accept this challenge?
- Should Queen Esther feel special because God chose her? Why or why not?
- What does it mean to have a purpose in life?

Princess Thoughts:
Ministry Leader will encourage Princesses to think about their purpose "at this very moment." Why are they here right now (this very moment), in this ministry, experiencing the life they have? What is God doing in their lives now? Do they think God can use them just as he used Esther?

STEP #4
Closing Activity: God's Workmanship
Princesses, feel the beautiful creation that God has made through us, limb by limb. Ministry Leader will ask Princesses to:
- Close their eyes and relax.
- Think only about right now.
- Wiggle their fingers.
- Feel their fingers—only their fingers.
- Slowly move different parts of the body, such as eyelids, little toe on left foot, bottom lip, right shoulder, etc, and focus only on that part of the body.
- Open their eyes.

Ministry Leader Final Insight: *The same way God took time to craft each body part is the same way he takes time to be involved in every detail of our lives. Take time each day* *to think about the very moment you are in, praise God for it, and think about how God can be glorified in it or through you; give examples.*

Closing Prayer
Ministry Leader reads prayer as Princesses repeat.

A Princess with a Purpose

Oh, Lord, I thank you for this day that you have given me. I thank you for this very hour, minute, and moment that I am in. I thank you for helping me to know how very special I am, and how you took time to mold and sculpt me into the masterpiece that I am. Thank you for my eyes, my ears, and my toes. Thank you for my birth. Thank you for the strength you have given me to live the life that you have called me to. Thank you for the smiles and laughter you've given me to enjoy happiness. For I have been created for this very moment with a special purpose.

Amen.

Session #5

A Princess Made Whole
God's Way of Letting Go

Philippians 3:12-13 (NIV) Not that I have already obtained all this, or have already been made perfect, but I press on to take hold of that for which Christ Jesus took hold of me. Brothers, I do not consider myself yet to have taken hold of it. But one thing I do: Forgetting what is behind me and straining toward what is ahead.

Purpose: Princesses will make a conscious decision to move forward in their lives by asking God to heal them of past hurts and pain. Princesses will experience the power of forgiveness.

STEP #1
Princess Imagery Activity: The Power of Releasing
Ministry Leader will ask Princesses to close their eyes and reflect on painful experiences that occurred in the past year. While all eyes remain closed, Princesses will call out "feeling" words associated with these experiences (such as hurt, sadness, and anger). As words are stated, Ministry Leader will write down the words on a large sheet of paper. Princesses will open their eyes and discuss whether or not this activity was difficult.
Follow-up Questions:
- How do our painful experiences allow us to relate to the experience of Queen Esther?
- What painful experience do we know Esther had at a very young age? *(Answer: Esther 2:7 Both of her parents were dead.)*
- What are some of the difficult experiences we know Esther went through so far? (Separation from her cousin, entering a harem, finding out about Haman's plot, etc.)

STEP #2
Princess Bible Study: Discuss Esther chapters 5-6, with emphasis on Esther 5:14.

- Queen Esther prepared something for King Xerxes and Haman. What was it? *See Esther 5:4-7*
- What did Haman's wife, Zeresh, tell him to do to Mordecai? *See Esther 5:24*
- How was Mordecai honored? *See Esther 6:6-10*
- What emotions/feelings do you think Esther had towards Haman?

- How do you think Esther felt as she made her request to the King?
  See Esther 7:3-6

Ministry Leader Insight: *Princesses will be encouraged to identify with Esther through all her struggles and appreciate her strength/courage. King Xerxes held power over Esther. She could have been thrown out of the palace like Queen Vashti, or worse, she could have been killed and her entire race could have been destroyed.*

STEP #3
Read Esther 8:1-3
    Esther 9:20-22

Princess Final Question:
After Queen Esther was victorious over her situation, do you think she was in need of healing? Take a few moments to discuss. Ministry Leader should introduce the concepts of forgiveness and growth, and the power of letting go.

Read Philippians 3:12-13

STEP #4
Princess Letting Go BALLOON Activity
Materials: paper, pens, balloons, helium tank
Ministry Leader will distribute small pieces of paper and ask Princesses to list the difficult areas in their lives that they need to let go. Princesses will fold paper and insert it into a balloon. Balloons are filled with helium and tied with a string. Princesses will have a private moment to release the balloon into the sky, symbolizing letting go of past hurts.

Princess Final Thoughts:
Princesses will gather together for closing prayer. Ministry Leader will request a Princess to read ***Esther 9:25-28*** aloud, and inform the Princesses that the next session will symbolize our celebration of Purim.

Form Princess Prayer Stance: Locking of arms
Closing Prayer

Session #6

Princess Purim Celebration
Ministry Membership

Purpose: Following successful completion of Princess Sessions one through five, Princess Sisters will receive their pins, read the personalized version of the Ministry Vision, and officially be welcomed to The Young Ladies of Character: Restoring the Princess Ministry.

AGENDA:

- Important: Princess Sisters will be requested to remain outside of meeting room until decorations are completed, allowing for a special entrance.

- Ministry Leaders and Princess Mentors with more than one year membership will decorate meeting room and chairs for Princess Sisters.

- Special pastries and beverages will be prepared for Session #6.

- Ministry Leaders and Princess Mentors will welcome each Princess Sister as they enter the room with the Ministry Princess Greeting.

- Opening Prayer

- Ministry Leader or Princess Leader in Training will explain purpose of Session # 6, and declare an official welcome to all Princess Sisters.

- Soft Instrumental Music is played in background.

- Ministry Leader or Princess Mentors will introduce the purpose of the ministry pin, which recognizes the completion of the first half-year of membership, followed by the pinning ceremony. Each Princess will be pinned with a Princess Membership Pin.

- Upon completion of the pinning, the Ministry Vision is distributed and recited by all Princesses, followed by a round of applause.

- All Princesses are invited to relax and partake of food and beverages.

Let the Fun Begin!

Princess Trivia Time: *NIV Used for simple language.*

Purpose: Princesses will remember and reflect on the book of Esther. They will be challenged to find answers in the Bible and remember the lessons learned by studying the book of Esther during Princess Sessions 1-5. The princesses will be evenly divided into two groups. If Princess Mentors are available, they should be evenly distributed between the groups. Each group will be allowed to use Bibles and will be challenged with questions from the Books of Esther and Ruth. Although a tally of scores should be taken to make this game competitive and exciting, the primary purpose of this activity is to remind all Princesses of what they have learned. If this is the first year of this ministry, ask questions only from the book of Esther.

Questions:
1. What were the names of the first queen and king mentioned in the book of Esther?
2. What are some of the events that led up to Queen Vashti losing her position?
3. Girls were gathered from throughout the province so King Xerxes could choose his next queen. What qualities did all these girls share?
4. Two part question worth double the points:
   (A) Who was in charge of all of the girls in the harem?
   (B) What process did the girls go through before being presented to the king?

5. What was Esther's real name?
6. Two part question worth double the points:
   (A) How were Mordecai and Esther related?
   (B) What life event brought Ester and Mordecai together?

7. What instruction did Mordecai give to Esther before she was taken to the harem?
8. What made Esther stand out among all the other girls in the harem?
9. What was the exact beautifying process the girls had to go through before being presented to the King (Read if needed)?
10. What did Esther request prior to her visit with the King?
11. Who was Haman?
12. Why did Haman dislike Mordecai?

Ministry Leader should continue to create more questions to complete the book of Esther.

Answers:
1. Queen Vashti and King Xerxes.
2. King Xerxes gave a banquet for all his nobles and officials. He displayed his wealth for 180 days and gave seven additional banquets in the palace garden. Queen Vashti also gave a banquet for the women in the royal palace. On the seventh day, King Xerxes requested Queen Vashti be brought to him wearing her royal crown in order to display her beauty. Queen Vashti refused to follow the King's orders. The King became angry, and a meeting was held to discuss what should be done in response to Queen Vashti's disobedience.
3. Beautiful virgins.
4. (A) Hegai, the King's eunuch. (B) Beauty treatments.
5. Hadassah.
6. (A) Mordecai was Esther's cousin. (B) Mordecai raised Esther because her mother and father died.

7. Mordecai told Esther not to reveal her nationality or family background.
8. *Esther found favor with Hegai (Important point: It was not simply beauty, because all the girls were beautiful).*
9. Twelve months of beauty treatments were prescribed for the women; six months with oil of myrrh, and six months with perfumes and cosmetics.
10. Only what Hegai recommended.
11. Son of Hammedatha, the Agagite who was honored and given power by King Xerxes.
12. Mordecai refused to kneel to pay honor to Haman.

Princess Trivia should end with a discussion of PURIM, which is still celebrated by Jewish people to this day.

Form Princess Prayer Stance: Locking of arms
Closing Prayer

Y.L.C.

Session # 7

A Princess Look at Friendship

Esther 2:9 (NIV) The girl pleased him and won his favor. Immediately he provided her with her beauty treatments and special food. He assigned to her seven maids selected from the king's palace and moved her and her maids into the best place in the harem.

Purpose: Princesses will gain a clearer understanding of the different levels of relationships we develop with the people in our lives. Princesses will appreciate the beauty and bond of true friendship.

STEP #1
Princess Activity: Let's Dress a Friend
Materials needed: firm paper (20in x 23in), markers, scissors, tape/tacks
Preparation and Activity:

- Ministry Leader will draw a silhouette of a woman's body on a 20in x 23in paper.
- Draw and cut out items of clothing and accessories large enough to fit the silhouette (ex. shirt, pants, skirt, dress, scarf, hat, glasses, etc.)
- Each item of clothing should list various characteristics associated with that of a "good friend" and a "not so good friend" (ex. compassionate, funny, attitude, loyal, quiet, jealous, gossip, etc.).
- Affix the silhouette to the wall and lay the items of clothing on a table.
- Princesses will dress their friend with the characteristics they think they would want in a good friend.

Alternative:

- Ministry Leader will clip articles of clothing from a women's catalog, magazine, news paper.
- Each item of clothing should list various characteristics associated with that of a "good friend" and a "not so good friend" (ex. compassionate, funny, attitude, loyal, quiet, jealous, gossip, etc).
- Princesses will pick their friends wardrobe based upon the characteristics they want in a good friend.

Dress a Friend Debrief:

Ministry Leader will encourage Princesses to share why they chose certain qualities for their friend?

(Princesses should be instructed not to respond to the following question, only think about it. Princesses will ask themselves if they hold the same standards when they choose friends in their everyday lives.

(Princesses should be made aware that we will go deeper into this conversation after we take a look at Queen Esther and the women in her life.)

STEP#2
Princess Bible Study: Read and Discuss Esther 2:8 and 9
- How do you think the young girls felt as they entered the palace?
- Do you think some of the girls may have felt scared, sad, afraid, nervous, or angry?

- Why do you think Hegai assigned seven maids to Esther when he chose to move her to the best place in the harem? *(SUGGESTIONS: support, friendship, company, assistance, etc.)*
- What kind of relationship do you think Esther had with her seven maids?
- Do you think some of the qualities you think are important in a good friend would have been important to Esther?

Purpose: Princesses will identify with Esther and the bond she developed with the seven women with whom she shared her life.   Princesses will discuss and examine how they view their relationships with others.

Princess Study of Friendship

Princess Questions:
- Do you treat all your friends the same?
- What makes you treat one friend differently than another?
  (SUGGESSTIONS: personality, commonalities, positive or negative experiences)
- What do you do when you have friends who have some qualities you like and some you don't?

Ministry Leader Charge: Let's make sense out of our relationships!
Ministry Leader will share the ideas below.

Princesses will think about the friends they have in their lives, and decide what type of friendship they are.

Encourage Princesses to be honest with themselves and explain that we often get hurt in relationships because we place friends in the wrong category.)
Categories/Types of Friendship:
- Cliques: Fake friendships consisting of a group of individuals who are insecure and who depend on one another to make themselves feel strong. People in these relationships usually hurt one another and the relationship only lasts if each

individual follows what the group wants. A clique often has a leader, although the leader may change based upon the group's willingness to follow her. The leader is often the most insecure individual out of the entire group, but appears strong by controlling/bullying others. A clique is a socially-acceptable form of a GANG.

- Associate: a person with whom you have general, polite conversations. You speak to this person, but do not make an effort to get to know him or her on a more personal level.

- Friends: a person with whom you have a connection. You maintain a relationship with this person by communicating regularly and spending time together or within a group.

- Best Friend (Intimate): a person with whom you have taken time and effort to get to know. Often your sharing of common beliefs and values makes this relationship develop naturally. This person has earned your trust over a period of time. This trust allows you to share secrets and insecurities. This person truly cares about you and will tell you when you are wrong and warn you when you may be harmed or hurt. You are truly blessed if you have more than one or two relationships like this in your life. These relationships are valuable and should be cherished.

- A True Christian Friend: a person who has committed his or her life to God, and who tries to live according to the Bible. This person may not be the friend you call to go shopping, but you may call on this friend when you are dealing with a challenging life situation. This person will share words of encouragement based upon the word of God or will assist you in getting the help you need.

Ministry Leader Insight: Each time we welcome into our lives someone beyond the category of an ASSOCIATE, we take a risk. However, God can use our relationships to bless us, so it is important that we build healthy relationships. It takes time to determine the type of relationship we are capable of having with any individual. Some relationships can also move from one category to another over time. We are often hurt when we try to treat an ASSOCIATE like a BEST FRIEND. We often try to place people in categories they have not shown us they can live up to.

Important Question:
Does a *FRIEND* or a *BEST FRIEND* have to be a Christian?
Can you really share everything with a person who does not live by the same beliefs as you?
2 Corinthians 6:14-16

What does the Bible say about Friendship?
Proverbs 18:24
Proverbs 17:17

Take a "Jesus" Look at Friendship: Read John 15:12-15
What does Jesus say is the difference between his relationship with a servant and a friend?

Ministry Leader Insight: *Jesus Christ himself takes time to point out the different types of relationships in his life and so should we. He clearly expresses that unlike his servant, his friend knows his business.*

Princess Final Thought: Princesses will reflect on the people who play important roles in their lives; the impact these people have on them (positive or negative); and the impact they have on others. Princesses will understand the importance of building Godly relationships.

Form Princess Prayer Stance: Locking of arms
Closing Prayer

Y. L. C.

Session #8

A Princess Look at Respecting Authority

Hebrews 13:17 (NIV) Obey your leaders and submit to their authority. They keep watch over you as men who must give an account. Obey them so that their work will be a joy, not a burden, for that would be of no advantage to you.

Purpose: Princesses will come to the understanding that God has placed authority figures in our lives for a reason. Although authority figures are imperfect people, just as Princesses are, they still should be respected. Jesus Christ is the ultimate AUTHORITY in our lives.

Preparation: *Ministry Leader must budget time to allow for individual prayer time at the end of this session.*

Materials Needed: STEP #1
Large Flip-Chart Paper, Markers

STEP #1
Princess Activity: Authority Figures
- Ministry Leader will ask for a Princess Volunteer to create two columns on flip chart paper.
- The first column should be titled "Who are the authority figures in your life?"
- The second column should be titled "Who are the authority figures in your parents/guardians' lives?"
- Ministry Leader will request the volunteer to list examples shared by Princesses on flip chart.

(Princess Volunteer should be positioned in the front of the room and write on large paper that is visible to all. As the activity begins, the Ministry Leader should encourage Princesses to list as many authority figures as they can.)

Follow-up Question:
- Based upon this activity, what do young people and adults have in common? *(Answer: We all have authority figures in our lives.)*

Ministry Leader Insight: *It's important to dispel the myth that when you become adults you will not have to answer to anyone. We all have to follow the leadership of others.*

STEP #2

Purpose: Princesses will identify with and gain a clearer understanding of those in authority. Princesses will also realize how their reactions affect the response of those in authority.

Princess Role Play: Role Reversal

- Ministry Leader will request Princesses to break-up into two evenly-distributed groups. One group will play the role of those in authority.
- The Ministry Leader will assign each Princess a role (parent, grandparent, ministry leader, teacher, etc.)
- The remaining group will play the role of young people (daughter, youth member, student, granddaughter, etc.)
- Ministry Leaders will sit on the outside of both groups and state a topic such as clothing, chores, choice of friends, or dating.
- Ministry Leaders will allow each group to argue their points from their assigned point of view/perspective.
- ***Each topic discussed should be a free flowing conversation. Ministry Leader should have minimal input other than to referee the discussion.***
- Ministry Leader will then allow the groups to switch roles and present more topics of discussion.

STEP #3

Princess Discussion and Bible Study:

- Why do you think God gave us parents and authority?
  (Ministry Leader Example: build and shape our character. Please elaborate.)
  Read Hebrews 13:17
- What does that scripture verse mean to you?
- What do you think your life would be like if you did not have parents/guardians who care about you?
- Did Jesus have authority figures in his life when he walked this earth?

Read and Discuss Luke 2:49-52

- What experience did Mary and Joseph have with Jesus?
- How do you think Mary and Joseph felt when they realized Jesus was missing?
- How do you think Mary and Joseph felt when they realized Jesus made the choice not to follow them?
  Re-read Luke 2:48.

A Family Discussion

- Do we ever hurt the authority figures God has placed in our lives, and how?
- What do we do when our parents hurt us or do not live up to our expectations?
- Is it possible to forgive such deep hurts?
- Why is forgiveness important? What happens when we choose not to forgive?

*Ministry Leader Insight: We never forget the pain another person causes us. We may feel forgiveness is beyond our power, but we **read** in **Philippians 4:13** that with God's help, forgiveness is possible. And through all our pain, God will be with us **(Read Psalms 34:18).** God did not intend for parents to hurt children or children to hurt parents, but sin changed God's perfect design.*

*A sign of true forgiveness is when you realize the pain caused by another person no longer has control over you. You are no longer held captive by these past hurts. True forgiveness allows you to move on with your life. **Read Philippians 3:13.** Real healing begins when we ask God to help us to forgive the person who has wronged us.*

Princess Prayer Time
Ministry Leader will encourage Princesses to find a quiet place in the room to pray for their relationships with the authority figures in their lives. Princesses should be encouraged to ask God to forgive them for disobedience and help to forgive those who have wronged them.

Form Princess Prayer Stance: Locking of arms
Closing Prayer

Y. L. C.

Session #9

The Royal Entrance of a Princess
First Impressions

Esther: 2:15 (NIV) When the turn came for Esther (the girl Mordecai had adopted, the daughter of his uncle Abihail) to go to the king, she asked for nothing other than what Hegai, the king's eunuch who was in charge of the harem, suggested. And Esther won the favor of everyone who saw her.

Purpose: Princesses will begin to understand the importance of etiquette and manners. They will begin to understand that etiquette is not simply a bunch of rules, but behavior designed to make people feel comfortable with one another.

Preparation: *Ministry Leader should review literature associated with what is appropriate and acceptable behavior in their culture/society. Ministry leader should be prepared to provide examples of appropriate forms of greetings, order of introductions, making conversation, receiving and giving compliments, non-verbal communication, helping others and so forth.*

STEP #1:
Princess Activity: Making an Entrance

Ministry Leader will ask one Princess to volunteer by exiting and re-entering the meeting room. Ministry Leader will direct the remaining Princesses to observe their volunteer when she enters. The Princess Volunteer is then asked to re-enter the room and take a specific seat at the farthest end of the room. Ministry Leader will then ask Princesses to share what they noticed/observed about their Princess Volunteer as she walked into the room (posture, stride, clothing, shoes, stance, eyes up or down, confidence, etc.).

Ministry Leader Insight: *Ministry Leader will inform all Princesses that their Princess Volunteer just made a first impression.*

Princess Discussion:
Ministry Leader will ask Princesses to share what type of impressions they give when they:
- Walk down the street
- Enter a room
- Have a conversation
- Answer the phone

Activity: The Royal Runway
Materials Needed: A runner, music
Ministry Leader will encourage Princesses to exit the room and practice re-entering the room by walking on the runner. Each Princess should have a chair in which they can practice sitting. Ministry Leader should encourage Princesses to have fun.

STEP #2
Princess Imagery Exercise:
Princesses should close their eyes while the Ministry Leader reads the following paragraph. Ministry Leader will lead the Princesses in a discussion using the questions below.

Reading: You have been planning for this special dance for a few months. This is a big day for you. You have taken the time to adorn yourself with beauty. You both look and feel great. You finally arrive at the anticipated location. You enter a room full of people you don't know. You search the room for a familiar face but seem to find no one. A person you have seen before, but do not know very well, walks toward you.

Questions:
- What would you like to happen?
  (the familiar person to approach and smile, welcome you, shake hands or hug, have a conversation, introduce themselves, escort you, etc.)

- Now stop and think; have you ever done this for someone you didn't know?

Ministry Leader Insight: History of Polite Behavior
Ministry Leader will explain that etiquette and manners change/vary from culture to culture, but are always designed to build relationships and make people feel comfortable. The word polite *comes from the word* poli *in French and means a polished person— someone who avoids roughness and who desires smoothness.*

Princesses Practice General Conversations
Ministry Leader will ask Princesses to share some topics they can talk about with people they do not know very well (weather, shopping, news, world events, sports, etc.) Why is "small talk" an important technique to develop?

Introductions:
- The first person's name you say should always be the person of highest authority.
- This person's authority is determined by business title or relationship.
- Everyone else is introduced to the person of highest authority.
- Avoid using the word *meet*; it places emphasis on the person of least authority.
- Gender does not impact the order of introductions.

(Example: Susan Davis, may I introduce John Smith?

Princess Reflection on Styles of Greetings

- Handshake: (Western Culture) Formal or business-like; a way to say hello, goodbye or thank you to people you've just met or do not know very well.
- Hug: Wrapping of arms around one another. This style of greeting is more personal and usually shared between two persons who have some form of relationship.
- Kiss: An intimate exchange between two people who have a friendly or romantic bond.
- Traveling Abroad: In some cultures, kisses are equivalent to the Western culture's handshake. It's important to observe acceptable behavior so as not to offend other cultures. You will have to determine what you can or cannot become comfortable with.

Ministry Leader will encourage Princesses to share which greetings make them feel *comfortable* or *uncomfortable*. Princesses should be encouraged to provide examples. Ministry Leader will show Princesses how to *AVOID* an intimate greeting from someone who makes them uncomfortable.

Ministry Leader Model: Ministry Leader will request a Princess Volunteer to try to greet them with a kiss. As Princess Volunteer leans in to kiss Ministry Leader, Ministry Leader will take a slight step back and extend her hand to offer a handshake rather than a kiss.

Ministry Leader will then encourage Princesses to practice different techniques to avoid *unwanted* intimate greetings.

STEP #3
Princess Bible Discussion:

Esther's First Impression: The Favor of God
Read Esther: 2; 8-9, & 12-17

Questions for Discussion:
How do we know Esther had both outer beauty and inner beauty?
(Answer: Esther being chosen is a clear indicator of her external beauty. Esther finding favor in Hegai's eyes (Esther 2:9), everyone that saw her (Esther 2:15), and King Xerxes' eyes (Esther 2:1) reveal the beauty Esther had to have inside in order to shine as she did.)

Is attitude important?

How does a bad attitude impact first impressions?

How should our relationship with God affect our attitude?

Ministry Leaders Insight: *Ministry Leader explains that attitude comes from the heart. People's self-esteem affects them differently. Some treat others badly because they do not feel good about themselves, while others put everyone before themselves. A healthy young lady has a good self-esteem and maintains a balanced attitude. It's important to care for yourself while valuing and encouraging other people.*

Final Questions:
- What can we do once we realize we have a bad attitude?
- Who can we ask for help?
  (Answer: God, Jesus Christ)
- What does it look like to have a Godly attitude?
  Read Galatians 5:22-26 (NIV) Fruit of the Spirit
- How might God help us to show a more positive attitude?
- Who is the only person we can truly control?
  (Answer: Ourselves)

Closing Prayer
Ministry Leader reads prayer as Princesses repeat.

A Princess Prayer Request

My Lord and Savior Jesus Christ, I thank you for the young lady that you have created me to be.
I realize that you are still molding and shaping me into your perfect design.
I know that within my own strength I cannot become that perfect woman,
but according to Philippians 4:13,
I can do all things through Christ who gives me strength.
Therefore, according to Psalms 139:14, I declare that I am fearfully and wonderfully made.
I ask you to restore my inner beauty so that I may share it with others.
Lord help me to make first impressions that are pleasing to you and find God given favor with others.
As I grow in you, may my attitude represent all that loves, is kind and true.
I declare victory in my ability to carry myself like a young woman of God
and continue to enjoy the beauty of my youth.
In the name of Jesus I pray.
Amen, and Amen.

Session #9B

Refining the Art of Etiquette
While Keeping a Servant's Heart

Exodus 2:5-6 (KJV) And the daughter of Pharaoh came down to wash herself at the river; and her maidens walked along by the river's side; and when she saw the arm among the flags, she sent her maid to fetch it. And when she opened it, she saw the child: and, behold, the babe wept. And she had compassion on him, and said, This is one of the Hebrews' children.

Purpose: Princesses will come to understand the importance of maintaining a servant-like attitude as they grow in self-esteem and refinement. Princesses will learn the basic foundations of etiquette and manners, and begin to practice them in their everyday lives.

Preparation: *Room Set-up*
This session should be held in a room divided into two sections. One space should be prepared for a general Princess group discussion and Bible Study. The second space should consist of a table with a minimum of two table settings. Chairs should be placed around this table. Copies should be made of the Princess Handout to be distributed.

Materials Needed: STEP #3
Dishware for an informal or formal table setting, which may include some or all of the following: Dinner plate, salad plate, soup bowl, bread plate, salad fork, dinner fork, dinner knife, butter knife, soup spoon, tea spoon, water glass, juice glass and napkin. Ministry Leader may want to gather books and provide more visuals to assist with this practice.

STEP #1
Opening Discussion: Princess Reflection on the Culture of the Young Ladies of Character Ministry
- How much time have we now spent together as a ministry?
- What is it about this ministry that makes you feel special each time you attend?
- Why do you choose to come back?
- What is unique or different about this ministry?
- What makes you feel welcomed each time you come?
  (special greeting, feeling of acceptance, comfortable being yourself, etc.)
- What are some of the things we do to make one another feel welcomed?

Ministry Leader Insight: *Each time we meet we serve one another in different ways. This service is designed to make each young lady feel special, appreciated, and welcomed.*

Follow-up Question:
Do you think it's important for Princesses to know how to serve others? Why or why not?

Ministry Leader Insight: *Once we understand who we are in Christ, we understand that the way we live our lives is an example to others.*

Let's take a look at a Princess who was a true servant and example to others…

STEP #2
Princess Bible Study: Read and Discuss
Exodus 1: 8-10, 15-18, & 22
- What did the Pharaoh fear about the Hebrews?
- What two commands did he give to solve this problem?
  (Answer: The midwives were told to kill all the young Hebrew boys and to throw every male Hebrew child into the Nile River.)
- Why didn't the Hebrew midwives obey the Pharaoh?
  (Answer: Exodus 1:17)

Read and Discuss: Exodus 2:1-8
- Explain what just happened.
- What did Pharaoh's daughter, the Princess, do for the Hebrew baby boy?
- What would have happened if she had not done this?
- What does this tell us about the Princess' character?
- Who eventually nursed Moses?
- What does this teach us about God?
  (God is in control; he is a protector)
- What did Moses go on to do?
  (Answer: Lead the people of Israel out of Egypt towards the promise land.)

Ministry Leader Insight: *As a Princess, Pharaoh's daughter showed a great level of strength and compassion in caring for a Hebrew child destined to die. We don't know exactly what happened, but the Princess had to eventually get permission to raise the Hebrew child, although her father had ordered the death of all the Hebrew boys. The Princess had the heart of a servant.*

Ministry Leader STATEMENT:
As we now begin to learn about the importance of etiquette and manners, we must remember that a Princess who keeps a servant's heart has the most impact on the lives of others. People who choose to follow her will know that her lifestyle and behavior is a great example of how they should live their own.

Question:

- Who is the ultimate example of how to live our lives?
  (Answer: Jesus)
- When we live our lives like God's Princesses, how might we impact the lives of others?
- How do we influence others to accept Jesus Christ into their lives by the way we live?

Ministry Leader Declaration:
NOW LET'S START OUR ETIQUETTE AND MANNERS WORKOUT!

Important Information
Event Planning

The Young Ladies of Character: Restoring the Princess Ministry within _____ Church/ Organization will begin practicing for the hosting of an event meant to provide members of the ministry with an opportunity to show etiquette and manners appropriate to their culture. The chosen event should allow members to exhibit the biblical Fruits of the Spirit from Galatians 5:22: love, joy, peace, patience, kindness, goodness, faithfulness, gentleness, and self control.

All Princesses should be required to welcome guests through invitation, conversation, and through "mingling." This event should provide an opportunity for the Princesses to share the ministry's vision, to share what they have learned, and to encourage others to join. The registration table should include a ministry signup sheet for the following year with a column for names and contact information. All guests should be served and made to feel comfortable. The event should be feminine in nature, but open to all. A form of entertainment such as games, ministry-related activities, or sharing of talents is important.

Original Event: Annual Princess High Tea Luncheon
See EVENTS section under Table of Contents.

Other Ideas:
Theme Party
Talent Show
Fashion Show

STEP #3

Etiquette and Manners: A Complete Mind Workout

Princess Discussion:
Ministry Leader should address each topic in the form of a discussion.

What is Etiquette and Manners?

Etiquette and manners consist of a learned appropriate standard of behavior that should result in people feeling the Three C's: Comfortable, Cared for and, wanting to be Courteous to others.

Etiquette and manners teach people how to behave in various situations, such as relaxed, formal, and intimate, based upon the relationship between those present.

What Etiquette and Manners is NOT:

Snobbery: Snobbery is a form of conceit or acting better than others. Snobbery suggests you are above others based upon race, class, gender, education, or some other trait. The purpose of etiquette and manners is to make people feel comfortable—the opposite of snobbery.

Only for the rich: Etiquette and manners consist of behaviors that should be learned by all people regardless of background.

A bunch of rules: Once learned, manners and etiquette can actually make us feel more relaxed in various settings because we know what to do and how to act. We also gain respect from others when they see we know how to behave appropriately.
Princess Question: Why do you think we gain more respect by behaving in a way that is mannerly?

Ministry Leader Insight: Guidelines for appropriate behavior have drastically become more relaxed over time. We are not under the same level of strict standards experienced by those who came before us. However, we must remember that we may not always be where we are now geographically; we may travel, or be expected to represent a major corporation. Learning these guidelines now can prevent us from experiencing embarrassing situations later, and help us to always conduct ourselves as refined young ladies.

Princess Reflection:
Ministry Leader will encourage Princesses to share what they remember from the last session and will incorporate those lessons into the upcoming event.

STEP #3

Ministry Leader Insight: *Ministry Leader will inform Princesses that we will now practice the etiquette and manners associated with dining/eating. (Please note that these standards are based upon a Western/European culture and can be modified if culturally needed.)*

Ministry Leader will hand out the following page.

Ministry Leader declares:

NOW LET'S START OUR WORKOUT!

Princess Handout: The Royal Dinner Table

Y. L. C.

Princesses' practice setting the table using the visuals and dishware provided.

Now Let's Take a Seat:
The way we sit at a table says a lot about the way we feel. Body language is important and also affects the comfort level of those we dine with. When sitting down or being seated (which is when the chair is pulled out for you), you should sit down gently until you have comfortably positioned yourself facing forward. Smiling at those you are dining with is always pleasant and expresses that you are friendly. If you do not know those you are dining with, you should introduce yourself.

Be aware of your body language. Throwing yourself into the chair, slumping, or looking at other tables rather than initially focusing on the guests at your table communicates that you do not want to be there. Something as simple as the way in which we sit down can leave a lasting impression.

Elbows On/Off the Table:
When first seated, simply rest your hands on your lap or on your chair's armrest. It's important to know your body. **If you are a person who has full control of your limbs,** once the conversation begins, lightly rest your arm on the table and lean in, which communicates that you are interested in the conversation.

If you are a person who often fumbles and has little control over your limbs, it's best to KEEP YOUR HANDS AND ARMS OFF THE TABLE. There is nothing more embarrassing than knocking over a beverage or dropping utensils on the floor, which results in needing server assistance and unwanted attention.

Conversation:
The type of conversation is based on the type of relationship you have with the others at the table. Close friends can have more personal conversations, but people who do not know one another have more general conversations, such as the weather, sports, the purpose of the event, and so forth. Remember to keep conversation light, but DO talk with one another. A quiet table is often an uncomfortable table.

Beverages:
At formal affairs, beverages are served. At an informal affair or at a tea party, it's okay to serve yourself by following a few important steps. If the pitcher or teapot is on the table and within reaching distance, simply serve yourself and return it to its appropriate place. If the pitcher is not within arm's length, ask the person closest to it to pass it to you.

Restoring the Princess Ministry

The pitcher should be passed with the handle facing **outward** for the next person to grasp. If there are people between you and the person closest to the desired beverage/or condiment, it should be passed to each person in between you. It is not appropriate to reach over people or push items across the table.

Reaching:
If you cannot reach it, ask someone to pass it. Do not reach over or across people.

The Food Has Arrived:
As a Host: At a formal dinner, the plate or platter of food should be served from the left as to prevent any accidents. Most people are right handed resulting in an impulsive response to the right verses the left which may take a person by surprise.

As a Guest: When your server arrives with your food, be prepared to shift your body in order to allow your server to place your plate on the table with ease. Be aware that dishes may be hot so avoid reaching for it unless you see your waiter is struggling.

Passing Dishes:
Dishes are usually passed counter-clockwise.

Dips and Dressings:
Use serving utensils to place a small amount on your plate. Do not allow serving utensils to touch your plate or your food, and never put anything into a shared dish that has been on your plate or in your mouth.

Refusing a Dish:
If you are served something you do not like or that you cannot eat, do not bring attention to yourself. When dining with friends, it's okay to refuse a dish with a simple "No, thank you." But if you have been invited to a dinner party by a host who has taken a lot of time planning the meal and the details of the affair, try sampling everything that is served (as long as it doesn't compromise your health). If you are allergic to a specific food, inform your host prior to the affair, or, if you were not able to inform him or her, do so a few moments after your arrival privately and quietly. Remember that the host has spent a lot of time and money preparing this meal for you, so it's important that you show appreciation. Once again: DON'T BRING A LOT OF ATTENTION TO YOURSELF.

THANKSGIVING AND BLESSING THE FOOD

1 Corinthians 11:23-29
Even Jesus Christ himself took time to bless the food. When we take time to bless and thank God for our food, we are thanking God for his nutritional provision and asking him to make it good for us to eat. It's important not to take for granted all that God has provided.

Now Can I Eat?
When dining with a small group of people (five or fewer) you should wait until everyone is served. When dining with a larger party of people, wait until a minimum of four people are served. If the food has not been blessed, wait. If you do not believe the food will be blessed, say a quiet prayer to yourself. And again, do not draw attention to yourself.

Holding a Knife and Fork:
Learn the correct way to hold a knife and fork. Practice using the correct utensils for the correct dishes. As a general rule, if multiple forks and/or spoons are provided, you will use the one on the outside for the first course. Leave it with the dish to be taken by the wait-staff. Work your way toward the plate, using the next closer utensil for the next course. If only one fork has been provided, keep it for all courses.

It's Time to Eat:
Most people like to eat. However, it's important to eat slowly and appropriately. Place a comfortable amount of food in your mouth—not so much that the food falls out or your face is distended in any way. Avoid speaking with your mouth full, and do not make loud noises as you chew your food.

Using a Finger Bowl:
A finger bowl is a small bowl or dish filled with a small amount of water. When you receive it, lightly dip your finger tips in it and continue passing it to the next person. Then use your napkin to dry your hands. Whatever you do, DON'T DRINK FROM IT.

Coughing, Sneezing or Choking:
Be sure to turn your head away from the table and cover your mouth with a napkin. If you cannot reach a napkin fast enough, excuse yourself from the table and wash your hands. If you cannot wash your hands, be sure to only eat the food already on your plate and only use your utensils. Do not touch serving platters, utensils or pitchers until you have washed your hands.

Mistakes Do Happen:
Don't bring a lot of attention to yourself. If you drop something, politely ask your server/host to replace it. It's important that you do not return items that have fallen to the floor back to the table. If you drop something in a restaurant that does not create a safety hazard, leave it. Your waiter or busboy will pick it up **later**.

Restoring the Princess Ministry

If you have been invited to someone's home, pick up the item yourself with a napkin and give it to your host. NEVER CRAWL UNDER THE TABLE OR A CHAIR TO GET ANYTHING.

Dirty Dishware:
If you are given a dish or utensil that is dirty, quietly ask for a replacement without drawing any attention to yourself or the problem. Do not tell other guests.

Something in Your Food:
Again, it's important not to make a big deal out of things and embarrass your host. However, you should not eat something if there is a hair or another foreign object in it. Instead, push the contaminated part to the side of your plate or quietly ask for a replacement.

All Finished:
Rest your utensils on the side of your plate; do not return them to the table.

The most important thing is to relax, enjoy yourself, and not embarrass your host or other guests. Be aware that appropriate table manners should make the experience of dining with others more comfortable and relaxed. As in all things, treating others how you want to be treated is the key. Do not do or say anything that will make your host or another guest uncomfortable. Never point out that another guest is not following the rules of etiquette. Be polite, but have fun.
God wants to take us to another level.

Take home Assignment:
Practice setting your own table at home. Be prepared to show your skills.

Let Us Pray

Basic Table Setting

1. Dinner Plate
2. Knife
3. Spoon
4. Fork
5. Napkin
6. Drinking Glass

Formal Place Setting

1. Dinner Plate
2. Dinner Knife
3. Soup Spoon
4. Dinner Fork
5. Salad Fork
6. Dessert Spoon
7. Soup Bowl
8. Water Glass
9. Wine Glass
10. Coffee Cup & Saucer
11. Bread Plate
12. Bread Knife
13. Salad Plate
14. Napkin

Session #10

A Princess Is the Heart of Her Heavenly Father
Deserving God's BEST

1 Corinthians 6:19, 20 (NIV) Do you not know that your body is the temple of the Holy Spirit, who is in you, whom you have received from God? You are not your own; you are bought with a price. Therefore, honor God with your body.

Please Read This Portion in its Entirety

Warning: Ministry Leader should gear this discussion and its details based upon the maturity level of the young ladies in the group. If your group varies drastically in age consider breaking the group up by age for this session.

Purpose: Princesses will come to an understanding that they deserve God's best when it comes to all relationships. High standards regarding relationships should also apply to the opposite sex.

Preparation: Plan time wisely. Allow first hour for Session #10 material. Create a box titled "Everything I Want to Know About BOYS." Create a small opening in the top of the box for Princesses to drop in questions. Based upon the size of your group, decide if this session will need to be split into two meetings to allow for a full understanding. It's important that this session is not rushed.

Materials Needed: Shoebox, paper, pens, laminating paper

Portion Completed

STAGE 1

Activity: All about BOYS

As each Princess enters the room, the Ministry Leader will hand them a piece of paper and encourage them to write down a question they have about the opposite sex. All questions should remain anonymous. Princesses will then be instructed to fold their papers and drop them in the opening located at the top of the box.

STEP #1
Princess Discussion: Setting a Standard
- What is a standard (definition)?
- What does it mean to set high standards for our life?
- How do we set high standards in relationships?
- What do you remember about the session we had on friendship?

Restoring the Princess Ministry

Ministry Leader Insight: Princesses should be reminded of the importance of understanding the types of relationships we have, as well as choosing our friends and best friends wisely.

- What does the statement "We teach others how to treat us" mean?
- Now, how does this statement relate to relationships with boys, either as a friend or a boyfriend?
  (Answer: Boys treat us the way we allow them to.)

STEP #2
Princess Bible Study and Discussion:
- How do you think God would want men and women to treat one another?
- Do you think God loves men more than he loves women, or vice versa?
  (Answer: No; Remind Princesses of our first session on the creation and the time God took to create both men and women.)
- What does the Bible say about how a man and woman should treat one another?

Read Ephesians 5:22-24 (NIV)
- What does it mean to submit?
  (Answer: accept, surrender, and agree)
- Is it easy to give in to someone else?
- Why is Ephesians 5:23-24 so important, and what does it mean?

Ministry Leader Insight: God makes a comparison between the husband as the head of his home and Christ as the head of his church. God explains, as the church follows what God wants, so should wives follow the will of their husbands.

IMPORTANT Question:
- Based upon this scripture, why is it important to marry a Christian man?
- How can a husband who is not saved lead us like Christ leads the church?
  (Answer: He can't.)
- So, how does God want a wife to treat her husband?
  (Answer: With respect and honor)
- Do we need to submit to, surrender, or obey any man/boy we have a relationship with—other than our parent—who is not our husband?
  (Answer: NO, he has no authority over you.)

Read Ephesians 5:25-29 (NIV)
- What does Ephesians 5:26 mean?
  (Answer: A husband should spend time discussing the Bible with his wife.)
- By sharing the Bible with his WIFE, what does *verse 27* say he is doing for her?
  (Answer: The husband is helping her to grow in God and to cleanse spiritually like Christ does for his people.)

Ministry Leader Insight (verse 27): "Without stain, wrinkle, or blemish" means our husbands should not wound us or cause us injury. This does not mean that we will never verbally disagree or have an argument; but it does mean we should not accept abusive, cruel or violent treatment. A husband who abuses his wife is not treating his wife like God would treat his people.

- How does *verse 28* say a husband should love his wife?
(Answer: A husband should love his wife like he loves his own body.)

STEP #3
Ministry Leader QUESTION AND STATEMENT:
Now, do you know any 13, 14, 16, or even 18-year old young men who can love you like that?

How to Check Out His Character:
Does he love himself?
How do we know?
Does he do well in school?
Does he take care of his body?
Does he do drugs?
Does he engage in violent acts?
Is he kind to others?
Is he a Christian?

Ministry Leader Insight: If a young man does not love himself or think highly enough of himself to try to do well in school, avoid violence, and say no to drugs, he will not be able to encourage you to reach your full potential or care for you. It's important that young men love themselves enough to make the best decisions for their lives.

This ministry is not encouraging you to start looking for a husband, but even if your parents have allowed you to have a boyfriend, these are good questions to ask yourself. The answers they provide will give a good clue to how he will treat you. Now, let's take a look in our Bibles at a man who was in love with a woman.

STEP #4
Princess Bible Study: A Biblical Example of Love
Read and Discuss: Genesis 29:13-30
What man was in love?
Who was he in love with?
- How do we know Jacob was in love with Rachel?
- How long did Jacob work for Laban to receive his permission to marry Rachel?
- Who did Jacob end up marrying first?
- How do you think Leah felt?
- Was Jacob the right man for Leah?
- Was Jacob the right man for Rachel?
- What did Jacob have to do to eventually receive permission to marry Rachel?
- How much do you think Rachel meant to Jacob?
- What do you think *YOU* are worth?

Ministry Leader Insight: You are God's special creation, you are his perfect Princess. You are priceless in God's eyes, and God wants his best for you.

Closing Prayer or transition into *STAGE 2*

ANNOUNCEMENT:

Session 11: Princesses should come to the next meeting dressed for an interview.

Y. L. C.

"Everything I Want to Know About BOYS"

Five Minute Break

Preparation: Ministry Leader will encourage Princesses to add any additional questions they may have in to the "Everything I Want to Know About BOYS" box. Ministry Leader will take a few moments to read the questions dropped in the box, and separate the questions that may be very graphic or better answered by an adult or mature Princess.

STAGE 2

Let's Get Started:
- Inform Princesses that as many questions as time allows will be answered.
- All question's not covered will be answered in typing/writing and distributed at the next session.

Princess Q & A: Everything I Want to Know About BOYS

An open dialog will now begin based on the reading of the questions, the follow-up questions, and all insights shared. It's important to cover the topic of abstinence and sexual purity during this stage from a Biblical perspective.

Recommended Scripture: 1 Corinthians 6:19, 20.

Q & A Wrap-up: Ministry Leader will encourage the Princesses to remember what they learned and to apply it to their lives.

Allow 15 minutes for closing activity.

Closing Activity Instructions:
- Distribute Princess Standards, pens, and a strip of laminating paper.
- Instruct Princesses to read the Princess Standards handout.
- Explain that they are to think of the HIGH STANDARD they will set for themselves regarding ALL relationships.
- Instruct Princesses to follow the format below and fill in the blanks.

Ministry Leader Insight: Encourage Princesses to think about what they are writing and commit to maintaining a lifestyle that is pleasing to God. Princesses should place this special declaration in their Bibles so they can be reminded of it on a daily basis.

Example: As God's Princess, I will treat myself <u>with respect</u>, so others will know to treat me <u>respectfully</u>.

Allow Princesses to complete this activity privately.

"Princess Standards"

Teaching others how I want to be treated.

Y. L. C.

As God's Princess I will treat myself

_____,

So others will know to treat me

_____.

As God's Princess I will treat myself

_____,

So others will know to treat me

_____.

As God's Princess I will treat myself

_____,

So others will know to treat me

_____.

As God's Princess I will treat myself

_____,

So others will know to treat me

_____.

As a God's Princess I will treat myself

_____,

So others will know to treat me

_____.

Session# 11

A Wise Princess Gains Knowledge and Understanding

Proverbs 1:5 (NIV) Let the wise listen and add to their learning, and let the discerning get guidance.

Purpose: Princesses will understand and appreciate that they were created with a unique purpose. They were given natural gifts and talents to be used throughout their lives. Princesses will understand that education is a necessary tool meant to build upon what has already been placed inside of them.

Preparation: Ministry Leader will transform the meeting room into a business office. A reception desk is needed to receive Princesses as they enter the room. A waiting area should be set-up in one corner of the room, and a separate area for interviews. The Princesses will interview one another, so line up two rows of chairs facing one another. Allow space between each set of chairs so interviews are private and not disturbed. Copies of "The Interview" are needed.

Depending on your choice of activity, please see section on "Career Development Activities."

Materials:
Poster paper
Markers

STEP #1
Princess Activity: The Interview
- Request that Princesses enter the room one at a time.
- Thank the Princess for coming on time for their interview, or inform her that she is late and can take a seat.
- Instruct all other Princesses to be seated in the waiting area and inform them that the interviews will begin immediately after prayer.
- Princesses may partake in refreshments as they wait.
- When the majority of Princesses have arrived, ask Princesses to link arms for opening prayer.
- Inform Princesses that they will now begin the interview process.
- Distribute copies of "The Interview."
- Inform the group of which Princesses will start out as Interviewers and which will start as the Interviewees.
- All interviews will be given seven minutes, after which Princesses will be encouraged to change partners and roles.

LET THE INTERVIEWS BEGIN!

All late Princesses will be instructed to take a seat in the waiting area, partake of the refreshments, but please not disturb the interviews in progress. Ministry Leader should walk around and see how the interviews are going.

Princess Activity Debrief:
- What was the interview process like for you?
- Did you feel prepared?
- What would have made you more prepared?
- How many of you remembered to dress for the interview?
- For those who were late, how did you feel?
- Which questions were you most comfortable with?
- Which questions did you struggle with?
- Which questions are illegal to ask, and the interviewee does not have to answer?
- How can you avoid answering a question that is not appropriate without being offensive?
  (Answer: Make a joke out of it or say you are not comfortable with the question)
- What is the purpose of an interview?
  (Answer: To see if you are the best person for the job)
- What is the difference between a career and a job?
  (Answer: A career is field you have chosen to study and seek to become employed in. A job is something you do just to make money.)

STEP #2
Princess Personal Assessment:
Ministry Leader will encourage Princesses to go around the room and share what it is that they would like to do and why. Ministry Leader will then ask the Princesses to share some of the things they do well (for example, fix things, do hair, draw, teach others, or give good advice).

Follow-up Questions:
- Why do you think it's important to like your career choice?
- Is your career interest based upon something you like to do or already have a natural talent for?

Ministry Leader Example: *There once was a young man who decided he wanted to become a computer engineer, but didn't like math. After two years of wasting his financial aid and his parent's money, he decided this was not the career choice for him.*

- What are some things you can do **_right now_** to become more skilled in the **_natural gifts_** you already have?
- When you find different ways to get better at the things you like to do, what is this called? (Answer: Education)
- What do some young people dislike about education?

Ministry Leader Example: *Ministry Leader will ask Princesses to give examples of different tools that are used to assemble an appliance or piece of furniture. Ask Princesses if they ever used a butter knife to remove or tighten a screw. What can happen depending on the size of the screw?*
(Answer: The knife may not work.)

Education is the necessary tool we need to successfully enter and grow in our career choice. A substitute will not properly prepare us with what we need to know. It's like trying to use a butter knife to remove a small screw.

Educational Point of View:
Education was meant to enhance and build upon the natural gifts that God has given us. Education should help us learn more about ourselves and draw out our natural skills. We should embrace every opportunity to learn, and always maintain a teachable spirit.

STEP #3
Princess Activity: Tips for Learning
Ministry Leader will ask Princesses to share what they do to make school/learning more enjoyable. Ministry Leader should request a Princess Volunteer to list the ideas mentioned on a large piece of paper and recommend that Princesses copy them. The paper should be titled as follows:

Tips for Learning

EXAMPLES

No procrastination

Good time management

Research topics of interest

Tutoring

Choose friends who get good grades

Study buddies

SLEEP

Stress Reducers

Please continue…

STEP #4
Princess Bible Study: Read and Discuss
Proverbs 1:1-7
- What was King Solomon known for?
  (Answer: His wisdom)
- What does *verse 5* mean?
- Why do you think God wants us to learn?
  (Answer: So we will be better able to do his will and use the gifts that he has given us.)

Ministry Leader Insight: The Bible instructs us to embrace every opportunity to expand in wisdom, knowledge, and understanding. So much so that the entire book of Proverbs was written with the purpose of providing instruction for our everyday lives.

Optional:
Read Luke 2:46, 47
Jesus Christ also understood the importance of education.

Final Instructions: *Ministry Leader should complete this session with one of the ideas below. It's important that Princesses leave this session feeling like they have a better understanding of their natural gifts and talents.*

STEP #5

SESSION IDEAS

Gifts and Talent Exploration:
Ministry Leader will provide and encourage Princesses to complete materials designed to help them gain a better understanding of their gifts and talents (See Session #11 Handouts).

Career Development Activities
Preparation: *Research résumé writing, photocopy résumé samples. Research and photocopy college preparation materials.*

Materials Needed: Pen and paper

Ministry Leader will lead Princesses in participating in one of the following activities:
- Mock-interviews
- Résumé writing
- College preparation

Guest Speaker/s:
(Please note that this person should be positive, able to hold your members' attention, knowledgeable in area of discussion, and open to participation. It's important that all presenters share experiences that are age appropriate, realistic, and encouraging.)

Invite guest speaker to come and share:
- College experiences
- Special topics (ex. time management skills, study techniques)
- Educational/career testimony

Video Presentation: Recommended Topics (Search your local library)
- Educational video from a world view, emphasizing the challenges the less fortunate experience in their quest for education
- Educational Video about the condition of education in your country, with a positive approach to young people.
- Career and Education video about career choices and/or institutions of higher learning.

(Please note that the video chosen should be interesting and age appropriate for your ministry members.)

Host an Event: CAREER DAY

Ministry Leader will lead Ministry Members in hosting an event designed to expose young people to the various careers available to them. Ministry Leader will recruit volunteers within your organization or community from various careers. They must be willing to participate for a day to share their career and education. This event should be designed to answer real questions about the pros/cons of various fields. Materials distributed should provide insight into career choices. Princesses can also participate in this event by sharing information pertaining to various levels of education, preparing those who are younger for what it to come. College information should also be available. This event should be open to the entire organization and/or the community in which it is located.

Closing Thought and Scripture Verse
Scripture Reading: Jeremiah 29:11

Jeremiah 29:11 (NIV) "I know the plans I have for you," declares the Lord, "plans to prosper you and not to harm you, plans to give you a hope and a future."

Ministry Leader Insight: God is concerned about every area in your life. Take time to pray about your education and future, and the direction God has for you.

Form Princess Prayer Stance: Locking of arms
Closing Prayer

ANNOUNCEMENTS:

Distribute Handout: Words of Encouragement
Distribute Permission Slips: Session 11B College Trip
Instructions: Departure location, time, return, etc.
Following Session should consist of taking Princesses on a trip to an institution of learning (ex. specialized high school, college, university).

Y. L. C.

Handout: Words of Encouragement

(Fill in the lines with your own creative words of encouragement.)

I know I can do this!   I am a very smart girl

_____   _____

If I work hard now I will enjoy life later

_____

It's cool being smart   I know I am college material

_____   _____

I can do all things through Christ who strengthens me!

_____

What The Bible Says:

(Search the Bible for additional scriptures to encourage yourself and write them on the lines below.)

Deuteronomy 28:13 (*NIV*) "The Lord will make you the head, not the tail. If you pay attention to the commands of the Lord your God that I give you this day and carefully follow them, you will always be at the top, never at the bottom." (Blessings of Obedience)

_____

_____

Roman 8:37 (*NIV*) "No, in these things we are more than conquerors through him who loved us."

_____

_____

Philippians 4:13 (*NIV*) "I can do everything through him who gives me strength."

_____

_____

John 10:10 (*NIV*) "I have come that you might have life and life more abundantly."

_____

_____

Pray and think about it.

Restoring the Princess Ministry

Career & Education Questionnaire
Session #11

The Interview

Directions: *The Interviewer will start the conversation by asking the questions listed under "Interviewer Questions." The Interviewee will ask the questions under "Interviewee Questions" when the Interviewer asks if there are any questions.*

Interviewer Questions

1. Tell me about yourself.
2. What position would you like at this company?
3. How did you become interested in this career choice?
4. What do you know about this career field?
5. How old are you?
6. Do you have a boyfriend?
7. What skills (good qualities) can you bring to this company?
8. Do you have any questions for me?
9. What type of salary would you like?
10. What can you tell me about your past volunteer or work experience?
11. Why should I hire you?
12. What would you say are your strongest and weakest quality?
13. Do you have any questions?

Interviewee Questions

Directions: Ask these questions when asked for questions.

1. Describe what it would be like to work for your company.
2. What is a typical day like?
3. Do you provide opportunities for growth?
4. What values/behaviors are rewarded in this company?
5. How do you see the company changing over the next five years?

Y. L. C.

Personal Assessment

Gifts & Talents:

1. What interests you?

_____

2. What do you spend a lot of time thinking about?

_____

3. What surprises you about your personality?

_____

4. What daily task do you look forward to?

_____

5. What do people say you do well?

_____

6. What do you do well?

_____

7. Do you look forward to learning new things, or are you more comfortable if things remain the same?

_____

8. What sports do you like to play?

_____

Education:

1. Do you enjoy learning?

_____

2. What do you enjoy most about school?

_____

3. What do you dislike most about school?

_____

4. What is your favorite time of the school day?

_____

5. What subjects do you like in school?

_____

6. Do you want to go away to college, or attend a local college?

_____

Career:

1. Where do you see yourself five years from now?

_____

2. Where would you like to live?

_____

3. Do you move at a fast or slower pace (be honest)?

_____

4. Do you enjoy the outdoors, or do you prefer to remain inside?

_____

5. Would you prefer to live in the city, the suburbs, a small town or a rural area?

_____

6. Do you look forward to waking up each morning?

_____

7. Would you prefer to work with others or primarily alone?

_____

8. List three career fields in which you are interested.

_____

9. What can you do this month to learn more about your career interests?

_____

10. What can you do this year to grow skills in your areas of interest?

_____

Y.L.C.

Session # 12

Beauty and Nourishment
A Three-Step Process for God's Princess

Esther 2:9 (NIV) The girl pleased him and won his favor. Immediately he provided her with beauty treatments and special food. He assigned to her seven maids selected from the king's palace and moved her and her maids into the best place in the harem.

Purpose: Princesses will gain a clearer understanding of the importance of caring for their bodies spiritually, physically, and emotionally, and learn how to put these techniques into practice.

Preparation: *Ministry Leader should prepare a menu of healthy foods such as fruit, vegetables, whole wheat bread and natural fruit drinks. Ministry Leader should take additional time to make the room look special by adding decorations.*

Materials Needed: Poster paper, markers, paper/stationary, and pens.

STEP #1
Princess Activity: Healthy Thoughts
Ministry Leader will distribute paper and pens. Ministry Leader will ask Princesses to write down what they think people mean when they say, "It's important to take care of yourself."

Princess Activity Debrief:
Ministry Leader will ask Princesses to share their thoughts. Princesses will list some of the things they do to take care of themselves. *As Princesses share, their thoughts should be listed on poster paper.*

Ministry Leader Insight: Ministry Leader will inform Princesses that there are different types of health, such as but not limited to spiritual, physical, and emotional.

*A Princess will be asked to **Read Esther 2:12**, and briefly discuss the beauty regimen Esther was put on prior to her being presented to the king, and why.*

Ministry Leader will then refocus the discussion on the three types of health.

Princess Questions:
- What is the difference between spiritual, physical, and emotional health?
- Is anyone more important than the other, and why?
- How does a person's spiritual health affect the other forms of her health?

Ministry Leader will inform Princesses that they are now about to have a detailed discussion about health from different angles; encourage Princesses to make themselves comfortable. If Princesses are seated on the floor, Ministry Leader should bring the beverages and food display closer to the ladies for easier access.

Ministry Leader Insight: *A woman's beauty comes from the inside. It's a combination of spiritual, physical and emotional beauty. In order to be healthy, we must nurture and strengthen all areas.*

Now, let's take a deeper look at…

SPIRITUAL HEALTH

A Princess Look at Spiritual Health
- How does a person become a born-again Christian?
  *(Answer: Ask God to come into her heart, **B**elieve that Jesus died for her sins, **C**onfess her sins to God, and know that he will forgive them.)*
- What are some things we should do to make/keep ourselves spiritually healthy?
- Why is our spiritual health important?
- What can happen if we are not spiritually healthy?
- What can we do if we realize that we are *NOT* spiritually healthy?

A Princess Look at Physical Health
This section includes a ministry leader insight (MLI) for each topic of health. However, it's important to allow Princesses to share their thoughts before providing insight. Ministry Leader should be sensitive to cultural diets and the limited control minors have over the food parents' purchase. However, it's important that they become more aware of their diets.

Ministry Leader should cover each topic below, discussing:
- ***Why spiritual, physical, and emotional health is important***
- ***What happens when we do not properly care for ourselves in these three areas***
- ***What can we do to better care for ourselves in each area of health***

The Basics:
Rest: (MLI) It's important to allow the body time to restore and revive itself. In order to function at your highest potential, sleep is needed. It's important to practice good time management skills in order to allow yourself enough time to sleep each night (eight hours is recommended). Suggestions for those who have difficulty sleeping: allow time for relaxation prior to sleep; pray about it; read a book; listen to soothing music; drink something warm that does not have caffeine or chocolate; avoid watching T.V. immediately before sleeping; avoid doing other activities in the location where you sleep. A person who has consistent problems with sleeping should consult a doctor.

NUTRITION

Healthy Eating Habits: (MLI) It's important to read labels when purchasing foods. Certain ingredients, such as saturated fat, coconut oil, and palm oil are high in fats and should be avoided when possible. Pay attention to cholesterol, fat, and sugar content. Eat small meals throughout the day instead of one large meal.

Meat/Poultry: Remove the skin from chicken; avoid red meat or eat it in small quantities.

Fruits & Vegetables: Eat lots of both. Darker/brighter fruits and vegetables equal more nutrition. Try supplementing junk food with healthy snacks.

Bread: Whole grain products are healthier choices. Avoid eating products containing large portions of white flour, as white flour is bleached and processed, resulting in a loss of nutritional content.

Dairy: Moderation is important. Choose low-fat versions of products. If you are lactose intolerant, see a doctor for supplements.

Junk Foods: Avoid eating; on the rare occasions when indulging, supplement with healthy snacks or eat in small amounts. Most people develop health problems when they regularly eat unhealthy foods.

The key is to do everything in balance. Too much of anything is usually not good for you.

Princess Questions:
- What is the purpose of food?
  Read Genesis 1:29-30
- Do you become tired after you eat?
- Why do you think this is?
- What happens when we eat a lot of unhealthy foods?
- What are some things we can do to eat better?
- What are some things we can do to keep our bodies in shape?

Exercise Regularly: (*Ministry Leader Insight*) It's important to exercise regularly. Exercising consists of activities that increase the body's heart rate, blood flow, and movement. This may be your walk to school each morning, activities during recreational time at school, or activities outside of school. Movement of the body is important for maintaining good health.

Ministry Leader Insight: The purpose of food is to nourish and provide our body with strength. It's important to be aware of what we put into our bodies.

HYGIENE

Feminine Hygiene: (MLI) As we age, our bodies go through hormonal changes that can result in strong body odor, increased sweat, bodily hair growth, and the beginning of a menstrual cycle. *(It's important to discuss all topics listed above.)* These are natural, healthy changes expected to occur in the body of a young lady.

Princess Question:
What are some of the things we need to do as our bodies mature?
- Cleanse ourselves more often

- Wear odor-preventing products
- Use menstrual pads and change them often
- Be aware of our menstrual cycle so we are prepared
- Groom ourselves regularly
- Determine facial products appropriate for our skin type

CLOTHING

Wearing a Bra: (MLI) It's important both to wear a bra and to wear a bra that fits correctly. If you have never been officially measured for a bra, go to a lingerie store or the lingerie department of a department store and ask a retail employee to measure you. Be aware that as you mature and as there are changes in your life and your health, your bra size will change. It's especially important for "well-endowed" Princesses to wear bras that give the necessary support to prevent back pain and other future problems.

Undergarments: Wear clean underwear at all times. Dirty underwear can result in a strong odor. Make sure your undergarments cannot be seen through your clothing. Generally, darker-skinned people are encouraged to wear dark underwear, bras, and slips under lighter clothing, and lighter-skinned people are encouraged to wear light-colored underwear, bras, and slips under white clothing. In other words, choose undergarments that are close in shade to the color of your skin to maintain a smooth flow of color under clothing. A contrast in shades will result in an unwanted visual of undergarments.

Personal Style/Fashion: Most people express their personality through their sense of style. It's okay to be creative as long as you carry yourself as a Christian young lady. Be aware of your body type and understand that every style was not designed for every body shape. The need for frequent adjustments of attire is a strong clue that you're not comfortable in your clothing. Be careful how much of your body you reveal; you may send the wrong message to others about the respect you have for your body and how they may treat it.

EMOTIONAL HEALTH

Princess Question:
How can you build your self esteem?

Positive Self Talk: Life is full of challenges. It is NOT natural to go through life without facing difficult experiences. However, the way we deal with difficult experiences is important. Say positive things to yourself to encourage yourself.

(For example, if you just found out you failed a test, say to yourself, "This was a very challenging test. I know if I study harder the next time, I will do better.")

Ask God to show you how to deal with a situation; talk to a relative or friend who you can trust about it; or search the Bible for an answer. *(Encourage Princesses to add to these ideas.)*

DO NOT put yourself down or accept feelings of defeat. Jealousy is the result of comparing yourself with others. AVOID comparing yourself with other people and be reminded that you are uniquely designed; you are fearfully and wonderfully made **(Psalms 139:14)**.

Safety First: Always make decisions that are in your best interest, or follow the advice of others who want what is best for you. Be aware of your surroundings at all times. AVOID participating in activities that may result in emotional or physical harm, for example:
- Associating with people who are risky or violent
- Attempting to form close relationships with people who have not shown you quality characteristics
- Suicidal and harmful behaviors such as but not limited to self mutilation or cutting; using drugs or alcohol; and being sexually active before marriage.

Wise and Healthy Decisions:
- Most people make decisions primarily on how they feel. Sometimes our feelings may lead us in the wrong direction.
- MAKE DECISIONS based upon your knowledge of what you know is right and what the Bible says.
- AVOID making decisions you know are not the best choices. If you will regret it later, don't do it.
- MAKE DECISIONS that are helpful to you and that will benefit you now and in your future.
- AVOID making decisions that will benefit others, but harm you.

Love Yourself: Always remember that you are a part of God's wonderful creation (*Princesses, remember Genesis 1 and 2*). It's important to make a conscious decision to love the person God created you to be. You are the only person with your exact fingerprint. God made you for a purpose. Take time to reflect on the characteristics that make you special and on the blessings you are experiencing right now in your life.

Ministry Leader Insight: *Ministry Leader should remind Princesses of the challenges that girls face because of the media and its misperceptions of what we should or shouldn't look like. Princesses should be informed that many young people die every day because of unhealthy body images that may lead to bulimia or anorexia. As Young Ladies of Character, we must understand that we are all unique in size and stature, which is the way God intended. It's important that we practice a healthy lifestyle and see ourselves as God sees us.*

Closing Activity: How Healthy are YOU?
Ministry Leader will distribute the following activity and request the Princesses to rate themselves. Princesses should be informed that they will not be asked to share their results, but participating in this activity will help them to see the areas of health they need to improve in and the areas they are already strong in. Princesses should be encouraged to reflect on the following handout from time to time and practice healthier living.

Form Princess Prayer Stance: Locking of arms

Closing Prayer
Ministry Leader should request three Princesses volunteer to pray for the ministry members relating to a specific area of health—spiritual, physical, and emotional. Ministry Leader should provide final closing prayer.

Y. L. C.

Directions: *Read each health category and check off the actions that you already do. If you check less than half (4) of the actions available to you, you are not healthy in this area. Make a conscious decision to work on it.*

Healthy: 4 and above
Unhealthy: Below 4

Spiritual Health

I currently do/have done the following:

- Made the choice to accept Jesus into my life (Salvation)
- Pray on a daily basis
- Read my Bible at least three times a week
- Go to church on a weekly basis
- Ask God for forgiveness when I know I have done something wrong
- Search the Bible for answers when I face difficulties
- Stop myself from doing things I know are not pleasing to God
- Tell others about God

Total: _____

Physical Health

I currently do/have done the following:

- Read the nutritional labels on the back of the food I eat
- Avoid or rarely eat junk food
- Avoid white flour and flour products
- Take the skin or fat off the meat I eat
- Avoid or eat small portions of foods high in sugar or fat
- Eat fruit at least once a day
- Eat vegetables at least once a day
- Exercise on a daily basis

Total: _____

Hygiene

I currently do/have done the following:

- o Wash my entire body at least once a day

- o Use deodorant or odor preventing products on a daily basis

- o Make sure I wear clean undergarments on a daily basis

- o Know what time of month my menstrual cycle will come

- o Wash my face at least twice a day

- o Change my feminine napkin often

- o Know my skin type and what products work best for me

- o Brush my teeth twice a day and rinse after meals

Total: _____

Clothing

I currently do/have done the following:

- o Wear clothes that are clean
- o Take time to properly dress myself daily
- o Wear clothes that are right for my size and body shape
- o Take care of my clothing by hanging, ironing, and mending them
- o Have developed my own sense of style based on my personality
- o Know my bra size
- o Wear undergarments that do not end up showing
- o Keep my shoes clean and in good repair

Total: _____

I currently do/have done the following:

- Say positive things to myself when I am upset or sad
- Know at least two scripture verses to encourage myself when I feel down
- Avoid spending time with people who make bad decisions
- Avoid spending time with people who encourage me to make bad decisions
- Avoid comparing myself to others
- Believe that I am a special creation designed by God
- Make decisions that are best for me now and in my future
- Avoid getting involved in behaviors that can harm me

Total: _____

Loving ME

I currently do/have done the following:

- Believe that I am fearfully and wonderfully made (Psalm 139:14)
- Do NOT make decisions that may be good for others but bad for me
- Think about the characteristics that make me special
- Thank God for creating me
- Thank God for the blessings he has given me
- Make the choice everyday to care for myself
- Teach other people how they can and cannot treat me (especially people your age)
- Ask God to help me grow in my relationship with Him

Total: _____

I AM *PRINCESS* _____, and

I am healthy in the following areas:

                          _____
                          _____
                          _____
                          _____
                          _____
                          _____

I am unhealthy in the following areas, and I will do better:

                          _____
                          _____
                          _____
                          _____
                          _____
                          _____

Young Ladies of Character:
Restoring the Princess Ministry

Annual Presentation Ceremony
AGENDA

Reading of Ministry Vision and Ministry Symbolisms & Meanings

Opening Prayer

Call to Silence

Reading of Scripture

Announcement of the Arrival of the Young Ladies of Character

Young Ladies of Character Processional
Princesses proceed down aisle and curtsy to their Ministry Leader, then take their place

Ministry of Song or Poetry

Princess Crowning and Pinning

Presentation of Bibles to Young Ladies of Character

Pastoral Word of Encouragement

Recitation of Covenant Prayer

Pastoral Prayer of Blessing

Presentation Announcement

"I now hereby present to you True Young Ladies of Character: Princesses"

Call to Applause

Recessional

Young Ladies of Character: Restoring the Princess Ministry
COVENANT PRAYER

Pastor requests Princesses recite the following prayer:

Oh, Lord, I acknowledge, accept, and declare that you are my Heavenly Father.

I accept you into my heart,

And thank you for dying for me.

I confess my sins to you and know that you are faithful and just to cleanse me and forgive me from all unrighteousness.

I solemnly promise to walk upright in you;

To spend time with you daily;

To whisper prayers to you all the day through;

To read your word so that I may apply it to my life;

And to share your love with those who do not know you.

I will conduct myself as a true Young Lady of Character,

Keeping myself virtuous and pure until marriage,

Caring for my body as the temple of the Holy Spirit,

And extending kindness towards others

And a helping hand to those in need.

I will strive to be all that you have called me to be,

And ask and allow you to guide my decisions in life.

Jesus Christ, I declare my love for you and commit my life to you.

Hallelujah. AMEN.

Pastor's Statement: You are now Young Ladies of Character, Princesses!

Young Ladies of Character:
Restoring the Princess Ministry

Annual Princess Royal Ball
AGENDA

Guests are seated and partake in appetizers

Princesses assemble for processional

Announcement
Princess Escorts are requested to join their Princesses
Reader of Princess Accomplishments takes her place at the microphone

Call to Silence

Princess Processional

Princesses will enter hall accompanied by their escorts. They will courtesy in center floor and form a line to receive their certificates. Escorts will be seated.
As Princesses enter the hall, they will be announced by name as well as the reading of three accomplishments of which they are proud

Presentation of Ministry Certificates

Opening Prayer

Call to Celebrate

Many Princess Members return to the ministry year after year; they not only enjoy the ministry but feel that it positively impacts their lives. Therefore, these sessions are the "next step"—an advanced series of sessions for those who have already completed the Princess ministry and are ready to become mentors. Please take time to read the following sessions before sharing them.

The Mentoring Sessions are focused on building the mentors' characters by challenging the young ladies to become an example for others. As the young ladies continue to learn about themselves, they are encouraged to think about how they can positively influence the lives of those around them. For example, Princess Sisters Session # 7 focuses on friendship. Princess Sisters examine how they choose friends and how important it is to determine if their relationships are healthy. Princess Mentoring Sessions maintain this perspective but also challenges Mentors-in-Training to determine what type of friends they are to others. The Biblical book of Ruth is the chosen text. The relationship between Ruth and Naomi is a perfect example of friendship, mentoring others by example, and the importance of building like-minded relationships. The beauty and strength of Ruth and Naomi's relationship is studied and made applicable to the lives of the young ladies committed to this process.

It's important as a Facilitator to lead these sessions in a more relaxed format. These young ladies already know and have a rapport with one another. The Mentoring Curriculum consists of six sessions, which are completed at the Purim Celebration. The remaining six gatherings should consist of community service projects, which may include feeding the hungry, visiting a nursing home, planning a special event for foster children, etc. Allow the young ladies to participate in deciding the community service venue for the remainder of the ministry year.

Following the completion of a year of mentoring sessions, these young ladies should be evaluated for leadership potential or continue participating in ministry events and community service. If a young lady decides to discontinue her membership with the ministry, it is her decision and she should be reminded that she is always a Princess and can return to visit. Young ladies discontinuing their membership with the ministry should be encouraged to become active in their churches. The most important aspect is that all young ladies continue growing spiritually and in character.

Enjoy.

Mentoring Sessions

Session #1M

Building a Mentor's Character
A Princess Reflection

Psalms 139:14 (KJV) I will praise thee; for I am fearfully and wonderfully made; marvelous are thy works; and that my soul knoweth right well.

Ministry Leader: This session is designed to simply find out how your Princesses are doing. This session should feel welcoming, celebratory, and relaxed. Princesses should be encouraged to share all areas of their lives they are comfortable sharing. This will allow Ministry Leaders to see how to best start off addressing your Princesses' concerns and needs spiritually and emotionally.

STEP #1
Welcome Back: Princess Mentor Discussion
- Ask Princesses how they are doing
- Debrief previous ministry year and events
- Discuss Princess presentation ceremony and its importance
- Discuss how Princesses have applied ministry values to their lives
- Discuss how the ministry's Biblical values have increased Princesses' spiritual growth

Princess Self-Reflection:
Princesses will share what they have learned about themselves through the ministry (Are they strong, passive, protective, kind, generous, have attitude, short-tempered, sensitive, or balanced?).

Question: How does understanding ourselves impact the way we relate to others?

Princess Reflection:
Ministry Leader will remind Princesses of ministry values learned as a Princess Sister.
(**Important Example**: We allow people to treat us the way we feel about ourselves. Remind Princesses how much time we spent talking about how special we are to God, how He created us, and how beautiful we are in God's sight.)

Princess Activity: Goals to Cherish *(Brief)*
Materials Needed: Index cards, pens
Ministry Leader will request Princesses list the areas they would like to grow in, and place the list in their Bibles as a reminder. Princesses should be encouraged to look back at the list throughout the year.

STEP #2
Princess Discussion:
Princesses will talk about their new roles as mentors and what to expect in this role.

Request Princess to Read Role Descriptions:

Princess Sister: Members of the Young Ladies of Character Ministry.

Princess Mentor-in-Training: Princesses who have successfully completed twelve ministry sessions and the Presentation Ceremony.

Princess Mentor: Princesses who have completed all eighteen ministry sessions and are ready to begin mentoring their Princess Sisters.

Princess Leader-in-Training: Princesses who have completed a minimum of two years of ministry and who demonstrate spiritual maturity and Christian leadership. Although maturing, this Princess should provide a Christian example of youthful living. This Princess should begin co-facilitating ministry sessions.

Ministry Leader Insight:
This ministry will continue to encourage all Princesses to understand and accept that they are fearfully and wonderfully made; in addition, Princess Mentors-in-Training will learn how to encourage others to believe this about themselves as well.

Princess Closing Activity: Princess Mentor-in-Training Rules
Materials Needed: Poster paper, markers
All returning Princesses will decide on rules to help them in their new roles.
These rules should not only be about themselves, but about the way they treat others.
Princesses should list rules on poster paper and display them at each meeting.

Princess Mentor Home Assignment: Read the Book of Ruth

Closing Prayer

Session #2M

Building a Mentor's Character
The Beginning Stages of Trust

Ruth 1:16 (NIV) But Ruth replied, "Don't make me leave you, for I want to go wherever you go and to live wherever you live; your people shall be my people, and your God shall be my God; I want to die where you die and be buried there. May the Lord do terrible things to me if I allow anything but death to separate us."

STEP #1
Blind Trust Activity: *A safe space is needed for this activity, such as a hallway or an open space with a few obstacles.*
Ministry Leader asks Princesses to pair up. One Princess from each pair will close her eyes and be led by the other Princess. Princesses will then switch places, permitting all young ladies to lead and to be led. Princesses will share their experiences in both roles, and determine which role was more vulnerable. Remind Princesses of new roles, and the various opportunities they will have to lead others.

Read Ruth 1:16
Mentor Question: What can we tell about the relationship between Ruth and Naomi based on this scripture verse?

Princess Discussion:
Ministry Leader will emphasize the importance of trust in close relationships, and open a discussion about what it takes to build a trusting relationship with others.

- How do you know you can trust a person?
- What are the characteristics of someone you can trust?
- Are you trustworthy?
- Have you ever betrayed a friend's trust?
- Must trust always go both ways?
- Is it ever all right to share a friend's secret?
- Is it important to trust the people who lead you? Why/Why not?

STEP #2
Princess Brainstorm:
Princesses will list various leaders' such as world leaders, personal leaders, or Christian leaders. Princesses will share knowledge of positive and negative characteristics of leaders.

Mentor Questions:
Who is our ultimate leader? *(Jesus Christ)*

- What makes Jesus Christ so great?
- What makes him the greatest leader?
- As a man, did Jesus always lead?

What advantage does a leader who had once been a servant have?

Ministry Leader Insight: If we look at the life of Jesus throughout the New Testament, we will notice Jesus had a servant's heart. Jesus could have placed himself in high places when he came to earth as a man, but he chose to be born in a manger. By placing himself in a humble family, he made himself available to all people. Encourage Princesses to think about the similarities they have with Jesus Christ. What are some areas they would like to grow in?

Princess Silent Thought:
As we learn more about ourselves, how do we lead by example?

Princess Partner in Prayer:
Princesses share a few areas they would like to grow in with a partner, and pray for one another.

Closing Prayer: Princesses come together and pray.

Session #3M

Building a Mentor's Character
Making Godly Choices

Ruth 1:7 (NIV) With her two daughters-in-law she left the place where she had been living and set out on the road that would lead them back to the land of Judah.

Preparation: Ministry Leader should prepare cards with topics such as boys, dating, hurt feelings, conflict with friends, peer pressure, sex, drugs, self harm, and other situations familiar to today's young people. Prepare multiple cards depending on the size of your group.

STEP #1
LIFE CARDS:
Ministry Leader will spread cards out on floor or table face up and ask Princesses to pick up cards that express situations in which they have had experience with, and hold onto these cards until later.

Ministry Leader will ask Princess Mentors who have read the book of Ruth to share what they remember.

STEP #2
Read Ruth 1:1-7
Mentor Questions:
Who are the key people listed in these first few verses?
What role did each of them play in Naomi's life?

Key People:
Naomi
Elimelech - Naomi's husband
Mahlon and Kilion - Naomi's sons.
Ruth - Naomi's daughter-in-law
Orpah - Naomi's daughter-in-law

Follow-up Questions:
What are some of the major challenges Naomi, Ruth and Orpah faced?

SUGGESTED ANSWERS:
Naomi's husband and sons died
Naomi had no husband to depend on
Ruth's husband also died
Ruth and Orpah never had children

Ministry Leader Insight: Clarify that the emphasis of these first few verses is on the loss experienced by these women. These first few verses set the stage for what is to come.

Brief Princess Discussion: Ministry Leader will encourage Princesses to reflect and share experiences of grief in their lives and how they made it through these painful moments.

Ministry Leader Insight: Emphasize the strength that it took to make it through these difficult life experiences and continue moving forward with our lives. Our society makes us feel that we have to "get over it," yet it takes a lot of strength to heal from a painful experience. Mentors should be made to feel good about themselves.

STEP #3
Read Ruth 1:8-18
Princess Discussion: Life's Choices
Ministry Leader will encourage Princesses to talk about the experiences that came to mind when they picked their LIFE CARDS. Ministry Leader will encourage Princesses to think about the impact their choices had on their lives, positive or negative.

Follow-up Question:
Did any of these choices have a major impact on their lives, and if so, in what way?

STEP #4
Read Ruth 1:19-22
Princess Question:
What were the difficult choices Naomi, Ruth, and Orpah had to make in this first chapter, and how can we relate to them?

Mentor's Final Thought: Ministry Leader will encourage Mentors to think about how the choice Ruth made took *their* lives in a different direction than if she had left Naomi. The choices we make in life can change the direction of our lives and those we have relationships with as well. Ministry Leader will remind Princesses of the importance of involving God in the decisions we make, simply by asking him for direction (give examples based upon the Princess experiences shared). It's important not to make decisions based solely on how we feel.

Princesses recite the following closing prayer:

Prayer of Decisions
God, I thank you for loving me so much that you died for me.
Thank you for taking the time to create me in your own image.
Thank you for caring about every detail of my life.
Jesus, I ask you to help me to make the kinds of life choices that you would want for me.
I ask you to help me remember to ask for your help when I am having a difficult time, and I ask you to help me hear your still, quiet voice when you speak to me.
God, I promise, when I hear you, I will try my best to make the decisions that are most pleasing to you, even if it's hard.
Thank you, Jesus,
Amen.
Closing Prayer: Should be led by a Mentor

Session #4M

Building a Mentor's Character
PERSEVERANCE

Ruth 1:19-20 (NIV) So the two women went until they came to Bethlehem. When they arrived in Bethlehem, the whole town was stirred because of them, and the women exclaimed, "Can this be Naomi?" Don't call me Naomi, she told them. "Call me Mara, because the Almighty has made my life very bitter."

Purpose: Princess Mentors will understand the importance of perseverance through difficult life experiences, and the power of speaking positive words over their lives and the lives of others.

STEP #1
Princess Mentor Reflection:
Ministry Leader will ask Princesses to share what they remember from Session 3M, Life Cards Activity. Ministry Leader will challenge Princesses to remember and explain the relationship between their challenging life experiences and the experiences of Naomi, Ruth and Orpah.

Read Ruth 1:19-22
Mentor Questions:
- What is the meaning of Naomi?
  (Answer: Hebrew origin, meaning pleasant)
- Why did Naomi change her name?
- What feelings made Naomi change her name to Mara (Hebrew origin: bitter)?

Princess Discussion:
Ministry Leader will ask Princesses why it's important to never give up hope.
Ministry Leader will encourage Princesses to share a challenging experience in which they were victorious.

Read Proverbs 18:21
Mentor Question: What do you think this verse means?

Ministry Leader Insight: Our tongue is a representation of a way to nourish ourselves. We are the only ones who ultimately choose what we will nourish ourselves with. We have a choice. We can choose what is healthy for us or we can choose what tastes the best, but may not be good for us. In life, we are faced with choices. We can make choices based only upon our feelings or we can make choices based upon what God would want for us.

Follow-up Questions:
- Did Naomi do what God would have wanted when she changed her name to Mara?
- Have we ever changed our name by giving up during a challenging life experience? What made you get back up and re-claim your name (figuratively)?
  (Ministry Leader will challenge Mentors to metaphorically understand that by giving in to defeat, they give up their name, just as Naomi did. Ministry Leader will then explain that when they decide to continue striving forward, they reclaim their names and the blessings God has planned for them.

Read Jeremiah 29:11

Ministry Leader Insight: *This verse is a confirmation that God has great blessings in store for our lives. It's important that we do not give up before we receive his blessings. When we receive his blessings, take time to be in that moment and enjoy them.*

STEP #2
Princess Questions:
- Who encouraged Naomi to persevere?
- Could Ruth have given up as well?
- What did Ruth do for Naomi by staying with her?
- Why is it important to have people in our lives that will encourage us?

Read Ruth 2:1-12
Princess Questions:
- How did Ruth persevere?
- What blessing of God did Ruth receive?
- How did Ruth's favor also bless Naomi?
- What happened to all of Ruth and Naomi's sorrow?

Ministry Leader Insight: *When we are in our saddest moments, it's important never to give up, never change our names. Many times we give up right before we receive our blessings. When we feel like we want to give up, it's important to have people in our lives who will encourage us to have faith and trust that God will be with us through the situation and will bring us out of it as well.*

STEP #3
Closing Activity:

"SAY YOUR NAME"

Ministry Leader will request Mentors move into their posture of prayer, forming a linked circle. Ministry Leader will then request Princesses unlink arms and face outwards. Princesses link arms again. Ministry Leader will lead Princesses in an activity in which the first statement is, "My name is Princess (name) and I answer to the name (a positive trait, such as 'beautiful' or 'intelligent')." This activity should continue until all Princesses have declared a positive title at least once. If the group is small, Princesses should have fun with this activity and continue declaring titles until they run out of ideas. Princesses should declare these titles with boldness.

Final Thought: In times of trouble, Princesses should choose to declare positive blessings over their lives and the lives of those who are close to them.

Closing Prayer: Should be led by a Mentor.

Session #5M

Building a Mentor's Character
Resting in God

Ruth 2:20 (NIV) "The Lord Bless him!" Naomi said to her daughter-in-law. "He has not stopped showing kindness to the living and the dead." She added, "That man is our close relative; he is one of our kinsman-redeemers."

Purpose: Princess Mentors will understand the blessing of having a close relationship with Jesus Christ. They will identify the victories and the blessings that are often taken for granted in their lives.

Materials Needed: Large drinking glasses (one for each Mentor), paper, pens, ribbon, news paper, and individual plastic bags.

STEP #1
Princess Mentor Reflection:
Ministry Leader will ask Princesses to share what they remember from session 4M. Ministry Leader will ask Princesses what they remember about the closing activity, "Say Your Name."

Life Application Questions:
- What was the purpose of this closing activity?
- Did you remember this session throughout your week?
- Did anyone apply it to her life? Give an example.
- How did this activity relate to the book of Ruth?
  (Read Ruth 1:20)
- As we read Ruth 2, what positive changes start to take place in Ruth and Naomi's lives?

STEP #2
Read Ruth 2:20
- What is a kinsman-redeemer?
  (A close relative of authority who family members can go to for help in time of need).
  Read Leviticus 25:25 & Leviticus 25:47-49)
- What does it mean to redeem something?
  (Get it back, buy it back, and exchange it.)
- Who are the kinsman redeemers in your life?
- Do you see Jesus Christ as your kinsman redeemer? In what way?
- Read the following verses and describe what they mean.
  Job 19:25-27 & Isaiah 43:1-4
- How do these scripture verses describe Jesus as a redeemer?

*(Jesus Christ, **"our original creator,"** will return to earth to **"take us back"** to heaven to live with him for eternity. While we are on earth, Jesus will care for us and protect us.)*

Ministry Leader Insight: *In the last two sessions, we spent a lot of time talking about the difficult experiences in our lives. Life is full of challenges; however, our relationship with Jesus Christ should give us hope in knowing that God will always take care of us. **Deuteronomy 31:8 reminds us that God will never leave us nor forsake us.***

Now let's take a closer look at the blessings that started to unfold in Ruth and Naomi's life…

STEP #3
Read Ruth 3:1-5

Follow-up Questions:
- What did Naomi tell Ruth to do?
- What was Naomi's reason for instructing Ruth as she did?
- In comparison to Ruth 1 & 2, what begins to change about Naomi's emotions?
- How do the roles of Naomi and Ruth begin to change?
- Who seemed to be the encouraging person between the two women in the beginning? Give an example?
  (Ruth informed Naomi that she would not leave her side. Ruth also began to work in order to provide food.)
- How does this change in their relationship relate to your role this year as a Mentor-in-Training?
  (Princesses are now challenged to encourage themselves as well as others.)
- What does the relationship between Ruth and Naomi teach us about friendship?
  (Friendship is important; true friendship should show mutual caring, respect, and encouragement for one another.)

Read Ruth 3:6-13
- What has happened?
- How is Boaz stepping up to his role as kinsman redeemer?
- Who do you think was always acting as their kinsman redeemer?
  (Jesus Christ)

Ministry Leader Insight: *If you have not yet done so, finish reading the book of Ruth for our next session. You will learn how Boaz truly fulfilled his role as kinsman redeemer. However, it's important to know that even if he had not fulfilled his role, Ruth and Naomi would have still been provided for.*

Jesus Christ is our ultimate kinsman redeemer. Many of us shared in our last few sessions the disappointments or hurts we experienced that were caused by friends, family, and/or other authority figures. Although man may try, we are imperfect people. Only God is perfect and will never fail us.

Final Thought and Activity: My Cup Runneth Over
The New Year is quickly approaching and we have a lot to thank our *Heavenly kinsman redeemer* for. We often spend a lot of time focusing on the things we don't have; let's take some time and focus on the blessings we do have.

Princess Instructions: Ministry Leader will encourage all Princesses to take a glass. Ministry Leader will place pieces of paper and ribbon on a table and distribute pens. Princesses should be encouraged to fill up their glasses with as many of God's blessings in their personal lives as they can. Princesses will be encouraged to decorate their glasses with the ribbon provided.

Ministry Leader Instructions: *When it appears all Princesses have written as many blessings as they can, Ministry Leader will ask them to hold their glasses in their hands. Ministry Leader will then ask Princesses to assemble in the closing prayer circle. Once assembled, Ministry Leader will* **Read Psalms 23 (KJV).**

Closing Prayer: Princesses will hold onto their glasses and volunteer to close out in prayer.

Final Instruction: Ministry Leader will recommend Princesses continue adding blessings to their ***"cup that runs over"*** as time goes on. Princesses will then be instructed to wrap their glasses in newspaper and take them home in the bags provided.

Session #6M

Building a Mentor's Character
Purim Celebration

Purpose: Princess Mentors will accept their first role of responsibility as a soon-to-be Mentor. Princess Mentors will appreciate and understand the importance of making their Princess Sisters feel special.

Mentor Responsibilities & Agenda:
Important: Princess Sisters will remain outside of the meeting room until **elaborate decorations** are completed, allowing for a special entrance.

- Ministry Leaders and Princess Mentors will decorate meeting room and each chair for Princess Sisters.

- Special pastries and beverages will be prepared.

- Ministry Leaders and Princess Mentors will welcome with the Ministry Princess Greeting each Princess Sister as she enters the room.

- Opening Prayer

- Ministry Leader or Princess Leader-in-Training will explain purpose of Session # 6 and declare an official welcome to all Princess Sisters.

- Instrumental Music should play softly in background.

- Ministry Leader or Princess Mentors will introduce the purpose of the ministry pin (recognition of membership and half-way first year completion) and begin the pinning ceremony (Each Princess will be pinned with Princess Membership Pin).

- Upon completion of the pinning of all Princesses, the Ministry Vision will be distributed and recited by all Princesses; a round of applause is due.

- All Princesses are encouraged to relax and partake of food and beverages.

Let the Fun Begin!

Princess Trivia Time: *NIV used for simple language.*

Purpose: Princesses will remember and reflect on the books of Esther and Ruth. They will be challenged to find answers in the Bible and remember the lessons learned during Princess Sessions 1-5.

Important: Princess Trivia Time will consist of a friendly contest between an evenly divided group of Princess Sisters and Princess Mentors. Each group should have a few Princess Sisters and Princess Mentors. Both groups will be allowed to use their Bibles, and will be challenged with questions from the book of Esther and the book of Ruth. Although a tally of scores should be taken to make this game competitive and exciting, the primary purpose of this activity is to remind all Princesses of what they have learned.

Questions:
1. Name four important people in the book of Ruth.
2. What tragedy happened in the book of Ruth?
3. What was the name of Ruth's husband?
4. What decision was Ruth and Orpah faced with in the first chapter of Ruth?
5. What powerful words did Ruth say to Naomi to convince her that she would not leave her?
6. What did Naomi change her name to, and what did it mean?
7. Where was Naomi originally from?
8. Who is a kinsman-redeemer? What do they do?
9. What was Ruth's first step towards recovery?
10. What order in Ruth, chapter 2, did Boaz give to his men to make sure Ruth gathered enough grain in his field?
11. What instructions did Naomi give Ruth to challenge Boaz to marry her?
12. What did Boaz tell Ruth he must do before he committed to marrying her?
13. Why did the closest kinsman-redeemer not want to marry Ruth?
14. What was the ritual symbolizing the redeeming and transferring of property?
15. As a result of the marriage of Ruth and Boaz, what king was born?

Answers:
1. Ruth, Naomi, Orpah, Elimelech, Mahlon, Kilion, Boaz, etc.
2. Naomi's husband and two sons died
3. Mahlon
4. Whether to stay with Naomi or return to their family of origin
5. Ruth 1:16
6. Mara; bitter one
7. Bethlehem
8. A close relative of authority whose family members can go to for help in time of need
9. Ruth went to work in the fields to get food for her and Naomi to survive
10. Ruth 2:15-16
11. Ruth 3:1-4
12. Ruth 3:12-13
13. Ruth 4:5-6
14. Ruth 4:7 (the transferring of sandals)
15. King David (but not for two more generations)

Ministry Leader Insight: *King David is a part of the lineage of Jesus Christ.*

Form Princess Prayer Stance: Locking of arms
Closing Prayer

www.ingramcontent.com/pod-product-compliance
Lightning Source LLC
Chambersburg PA
CBHW080243270326
41926CB00020B/4352